Theology
and the Church
in the
University

Theology and the Church in the University

by JULIAN N. HARTT

Philadelphia
THE WESTMINSTER PRESS

STANDARD BOOK No. 664-24845-4

LIBRARY OF CONGRESS CATALOG CARD No. 69-14198

PUBLISHED BY THE WESTMINSTER PRESS ®
PHILADELPHIA, PENNSYLVANIA

PRINTED IN THE UNITED STATES OF AMERICA

Dedicated to the the memory of
  Kenneth W. Underwood (1919–1968)
Vision, Fidelity, Courage: In rare compact these were the
  measure of the man

Preface

Some of the material of this essay was first presented as Danforth Lectures given at Brown University in the academic year 1964–1965. I wish to express my appreciation to the then president of that university, Dr. Barnaby Keeney, for the opportunity thus provided to think on these things. The chaplain of Brown University, the Reverend Charles Baldwin, is to be thanked for his encouragement at every turn. Prof. Kenneth Underwood unstintingly shared with me results of his massive study of the church on the campus. I have benefited profoundly from the years of association with him in pursuit of common interests. Finally my wife, Neva B. Hartt, remains the most constant source of support in sickness and in health, and I am happy to make public acknowledgment of this fact.

There are many issues and there is a great deal of discussion of these issues in print to none of which have I made allusion in this essay. Accordingly not even by the most generous definition of terms could this be regarded as a contribution to scholarship in higher education. My concerns are very largely theological. The times are interesting and perhaps critical for theology (as they are for the church), and there is no indication that the college chapel is in a fair way to avoid the theological and ethical testing that the church elsewhere is undergoing. Indeed the chapel on the campus seems to be feeling many of the bumps first. This is the situation I have tried to explore theologically.

Life nowadays in the university is rarely dull. Turmoil is hardly an infallible presage of the dawn of a creative age for university and society, but it is not an overwhelming argument against the arrival of such an age either. Some of the turmoil on the campus directly echoes events in the macrocosmic society and is probably an extension of such. But some of the turbulence is generated by frustrations and anxieties largely unique to the campus. Among the former many would list galloping disenchantment with many of the historic institutions of the nation as well as with the leadership of the same. Among the latter many would list as of paramount significance an explicit clash of fundamental outlooks — theologies, I suppose we could call them. The campus atmosphere is heavily charged with frustration over the ways in which these important conflicts have been blunted, muted, and papered over. It is a sad and perhaps a silly mistake to construe this as an aspect of the generation gap and particularly as an exacerbated form of adolescent rejection of parental or parental-like authority. What is at stake is not really who is to govern, in the university as well as elsewhere, but for whom and how they are to govern, and what are the rights of dissidence in the modifying of institutional policies. The great divisions on these matters do not respect generational lines, at least in the university.

I do, indeed, believe that a profoundly creative age may be just ahead of us, for the university and for much else in this society. It is not coming this way on the tracks of a world-historical dialectical trolley. The future is open. This means that part of the price for a renewal of creativity is great travail, accepted in freedom. The balance of the price is composed of such elements as lucidity of aim, wisdom in instrumental decision, courage to do the unpopular thing when it is necessary to the aims lucidly envisaged, and steadfast hope. A very large order, but the game has very large stakes. Then why not work as well as hope for the best?

The college chapel may yet prove to be in a strategic situation to illuminate the conflicts in American society, beginning with the university, and — a larger dream — to offer significant help in the constructive resolution of these conflicts. To this end we ought to pray, " God send us men," for the pews as well as for the pulpit.

J.N.H.

Sioux Falls, South Dakota
August 13, 1968

Contents

Introduction

I

This essay is not advanced as a feat of prophecy. The future is undoubtedly full of surprises, wonderful, trivial, and horrid. Lacking real prophetic gifts and a keen desire to face things before they must be faced, we can agree to use "prospects" in a nonprophetic manner, that is, as a way of calling attention to things sharing time present with us and worthy of thinking about.

In this essay I have tried to think about the university as a unique arena for theological argument. I have tried to think about this as a theologian rather than as a philosopher or sociologist or psychologist or historian or educational specialist. Moreover, the theological mode in which this reflection is cast is dogmatic. To identify it may have the sole virtue of drawing the lightning very early in the day rather than encouraging it to accumulate, for surely the lightning is there ready to explode against any curb upon freedom of inquiry and freedom of speech and against any suggestion that open-endedness might not be the supreme virtue of any rational world view. Are we then to suffer a plea for the benefits of dogmatism? Hardly. What element of traditional Christian outlook is more intransigent than the belief that man in all his ways and until the end of time is fallible, no matter how cleverly he tinkers with his environment or how far he extends his mortal years — as a place and time in which to make ever more ruinous mistakes? Granted that one can be dogmatic about this rather than open-ended, but can that matter so greatly as our really knowing that man always has made and always will make mistakes? Or is it the plain counsel of reason that we ought to be open to the possibility that in due time man, or some men, will cease to be fallible? That would be strange counsel indeed. What confidence could we thereafter have in reason, this ennobling capacity of man, anciently celebrated as itself divine, or at least godlike, once it delivered an oracle so profitless for present instruction?

What then is proposed here as a dogmatic theological perspective? Simply a perspective defined by acceptance as true of certain traditional teachings of the Christian church. These teachings yield implications of more general interest than the formal teachings themselves — I mean of greater interest to people generally rather than to professional theologians. For their part professional theologians are rarely committed to trying to make theologians out of dedicated church people. But the business of bringing the people of the church to face and to appropriate the proper material inferences of their religious beliefs is surely one of the best ways of getting them to understand these beliefs. Once so understood, these beliefs may be repudiated so far as any practical effect is concerned. This kind of unbelief ought not to be confused with the reflective rejection of the Christian outlook on the grounds that it is hopelessly at odds with the realities of the human predicament in the world.

II

To ask about the prospects of the church in the university is not to ask about the prospects of the Christian university. Nevertheless, something may be gained by a brief

16

inspection of the latter issue even though we may wonder whether it now agitates anyone except students aroused by the heinous affront to spiritual freedom and intellectual honesty offered by the sight of the Christian chapel (even though it may be equipped with a retractable cross) in the geographical heart of the campus. Accordingly I propose to review certain conceptions of the factors and qualities that heretofore have induced reasonably intelligent and responsible people to advertise a university as Christian.

1. A university is Christian if it preserves significant elements of Christian worship and Christian belief as a significant and formal commitment of the university as such. A Christian chapel supported by the university would be such an element. Regular courses in Christian beliefs would be another such element — whether or not the faculty motivation in offering and in teaching such courses was evangelical. Courses in the history of Christian institutions would not necessarily be such an element, since they could with some plausibility be offered under the rubric of Successful Errors, or, Mistakes Man Need Not Make Forever.

2. Obedience to a Christian ecclesiastical society is sometimes taken to be a proper and sufficient reason for identifying a university as Christian. As matters now stand this is hardly good for anything but sociological identification, and it works as well for hospitals and orphanages as it does for schools and colleges. At best it tells us who pays the bills.

That is of course an exaggeration, but it is not a fantastic one. It is reasonable to expect that ecclesiastical management of an institution would evince a serious religious intent. So if a church owns a college, it might well be committed to religious education of a sort compatible with the faith and life of that church. This was once undoubtedly the case with church-related schools. It is no longer so of most of them. Ecclesiastical control of higher education in the Protestant sector is vestigial at most. The churches no longer pay the bills, and so the schools nominally related to

17

churches have had independence thrust upon them, whether or not it has been passionately sought by someone calling the signals. Headquarters continue to list great and near-great universities as part of the empire. The real decisions are made locally, with the help of Washington.

3. But we have yet to speak of something much nearer the heart of the matter: Christian attitudes, values, and morals. In the flush of freedom from ecclesiastical domination and dogmatic rigidity, and in the first heady draft of idealistic amiability, people of the church have identified attitudes as their chief concern in higher education, if not in everything. But I think we can afford to be suspicious about this expansive mentality, given the facts. Institutional commitment to attitudes, values, and morals is mostly a matter of catalog piety and other forms of advertising. To put it thus is not an invitation to cynicism. Attitudes and values are not generated by decree or proclamation. A legal-moral code can of course be decreed together with stated penalties for breaking the rules. Against this fact it simply will not do to push the tired old saw, " You can't legislate people into righteousness." A society that will not announce and enforce the basic ground rules for its persistence as a society has no moral claims upon the loyalty of its constituents, and as such it has no moral reality at all. So it is not likely that universities generally are about to dispense with every kind of legal-moral code, even though the tides are running strongly against parietal rules. But is there any good reason for calling such codes Christian? " Thou shalt not cheat " is a fundamental ground rule in the academic community. A person who breaks it has no significant claim upon that school except a decent good-by — he cannot rightly sue even for an honorable discharge, whatever the department of university health may say about his unhappy childhood. But, again, the indispensability of that rule is no warrant for labeling it " Christian." It is a rule of the " lower righteousness ": its provenance is the minimum re-

quirements of the health of the community. It may therefore be likened to a sanitation code. Without knowing a
thing about germs, the ancient Israelites stumbled upon
some of the basic sanitation requirements for safeguarding
the health of the communtiy. This does not mean that the
sanitation code in Leviticus needs to be treated as though
it were part of the revelation of God to Moses. Neither is
" Thou shalt not cheat " an organic part of the "higher
righteousness " disclosed in Jesus Christ.

I do not mean to trivialize the role of the university as a
teacher of morals. Beyond its unique demands there are the
moral claims of the macrocosmic society. Is the Christian
college not best seen as a unique training ground for a morally sound life in that world?

Questions like this seem to spring from an assumption
that the wider world itself makes specifically Christian demands. This assumption betrays the presence of old linguistic habits of which none seems less curable than " the
Judeo-Christian tradition." This linguistic habit is the product of a disposition to believe that the central institutions
of American culture are the direct outgrowths of Biblical
religion, and that Biblical religion is a miraculous synthesis of the important elements of the Old Testament, the
New Testament, and the best of pagan civilization. This is
a religious claim. More properly, it is a claim made about
religion and it deserves scrutiny. Here I want to file a demurrer against the popular conception of the ethical responsibilities of the Christian university, as follows:

The university that undertakes as part of its contract to
inculcate sound Christian morals is very likely to find itself
committed to things that are formidable obstacles to the
attainment of essential Christian attitudes and to the understanding of fundamental Christian beliefs. These obstacles
are: a parochial understanding of the Christian moral life,
and an authoritarian ecclesiastical control of campus life.

By " parochial " I mean an arbitrarily foreshortened representation of the ethical community in which the Christian has a unique vocation. We ought not to object to a system of morals because it is made up of particular and specific obligations rather than of broad directives, injunctions, and idealizations. Any viable system of morals is steeped in particularity. But some systems illicitly proceed from such particularity to shrink the boundaries of the ethical community and thereafter draw the lineaments of the persons to whom I am morally bound after the likeness of myself and my ingroup. So the church is always having to fight parochialism in its own life. The higher righteousness is often the loser in this conflict. And from it my " brother " emerges as the person who has met the arbitrary qualifications for membership in the cult, despite the fact that the parable of the good Samaritan is treasured as part of the revelation of the cult.

As for " authoritarian " ecclesiastical control of campus life, I think it is reasonable, if not sufficient, to note that as a model of human organization it is explicitly rejected by that divine representative of the higher righteousness, Jesus Christ himself. This rejection has been greatly softened by interpretation confronted by the harsh necessities of history. This is to say that students are generally, if not predictably, immature and must therefore be firmly guided into the paths of righteousness. Is this a sound reason for treating faculty, too, as though they were fractious and impulsive children?

These considerations should lead us to theological arguments about the ethical community, the structure of the church, and the ends of the university. Such, in fact, are the objectives of this essay. As a way into these arguments I propose to discuss the relation of commitment and criticism to each other in the academic community.

Theology
and the Church
in the
University

Chapter One

CHRISTIAN COMMITMENT
AND THE CRITICAL LIFE

I

What is the university? The affective context of the question is now turmoil, incertitude, and foreboding rather than the philosophic tranquillity in which it was once asked and answered. Change has caught up with the university, and it has become the intellectual redoubt of revolution. No wonder there is much viewing with alarm and little pointing with pride, except in the offices of admissions and development.

Among many others there are two aspects of this situation that merit early and close attention. To attend to them will hardly guarantee a clear and persuasive answer to the initial question. To do so, nonetheless, may assist us as we struggle to understand what is happening to the university and how the church should respond to these developments.

The first of these aspects of the current scene is the chasm that has opened between the major components of the university, the students and the faculty. (I do not mean thereby to slight administrators and trustees — they have their reward.) The second aspect is a profound disagreement over that end of the university hitherto identified as the rational life. I shall consider these in the order of their appearance here.

Now surely one ought to expect to discover in the university some of the standard tensions between an adult generation invested with authority and a young generation obliged to adjust to it. Tensions of this order are commonly understood, if not enjoyed, as simple, inescapable facts of life. As a surrogate parent, as boss in a home away from home, the adult sector of the university can count on being the target of resentment, thinly disguised hostility, and open rebellion. Today's students are devoutly committed to seeing that these expectations are not cheated of fulfillment. But this is an old story. Where is an element of novelty, apart from the bizarre extremes of student protest? Real novelties are not far to seek.

Consider, for instance, the tensions generated by the global character of the university. An institution is global when it encompasses both trivial and definitive elements of the daily life of its members. The university is well on its way to becoming this kind of institution in American life. It is very rapidly losing the general aspect of an institution ancillary to more massive and more imperial structures. Some still speak of it as a service facility, but this talk is seriously misleading if it really bespeaks a notion, or a hope, that the university has not yet achieved autonomy. It has in fact become an empire among empires.

But has not the university always been global, always, that is, in the experience of even the oldest hands on the place? Does it not seem that going to college has always meant stepping from one global institution into another with every expectation that having taken that momentous step, at once exhilarating and frightening, one would not be able to go home again? The life-style would be altered. One was there to learn how to belong to oneself, and the way into that was to belong to one's college. This is what it meant to go to college, even to the most obscure school in the vast cultural wilderness west of the Hudson that had wangled the name of university from legislators innocent of any knowledge of the real thing. The college was the world in which we lived: there we worked, ate, slept, loved, and sometimes thought. College was a way of life, for better and for worse. College was Alma Mater indeed. It was more than the beginning of a new life. It was a paradigm of the good life.

In those halcyon years, we were the college. But not in some consciously excluding sense; rather, in the simple sense that we lived there while the adults had lives elsewhere: wives and children to look after, civic causes to serve, churches to pastor, farms to tend. Theirs was the great world outside, and they were welcome to it. Our world was intramural — near, dear, and all too quickly sped. O bright college years.

How vastly different is the present scene! This is the age of the multiversity. Paradoxically this incredible evolution of the university seems to explode any remaining pretension that it is still a global institution. Its administrators have become educational brokers supervising the investment of marginal capital, i.e., the on-campus time of the faculty, in the intellectual life of the students, many of whom are as fully engaged in the great world outside as are their titular mentors. Universities in which faculty time is not under heavy and attractive solicitation from business, government, etc., have become increasingly dependent upon students who have little interest in making college a way of life. Every type and quality of university is having to live with students who have had little experience with any global institution other than the structures of public education. This is a system that is not notorious for its power to develop strong loyalties to itself, a weakness it appears to share with the middle-class family. These antecedent institutions are supposed to have fostered values and sound values at that. Perhaps they have and perhaps they have not. In any case the adult generation cannot assume that students share the goals and the criteria of the people who teach in the university. The tensions between the generations in the university are no longer generated by agreement on aims and disagreement over means. Everywhere one senses dubiety, at least, about the whole inherited system of value — means and ends and venerable theories about how means and ends are to be understood in relation to each other.

Thus pretty much across-the-board students are likely to assay the quality of college life with criteria derived either from nonacademic experience and institution or from the exigencies of the interior subjective world. They demand on-campus privileges guaranteed by the Constitution of the United States rather than by the board of regents or the faculty. But they also reserve the right to break laws — federal, state, municipal, and academic — where freedom or justice is at stake. And in so doing, they appeal to Constitution or to conscience or to the revealed will of God or to the moral sensibilities of all men of honor, as the case warrants, and whether or not today's appeal is consistent with yesterday's. What decent soul will worry about consistency while the world is marked for burning?

What then has happened to that ideal of the university conventionally identified as the rational life? Around this aspect of the university angry clouds of conflict also swirl. But that of course is not a good reason for surrendering the ideal. There are many immoralities in the conduct of public affairs. It is proper to raise the hue and cry against them, and in this pursuit old antagonisms between faculty and students may be allayed for the moment. But surely the university is something else before it becomes the latter-day prophet thundering judgment against wickedness in high places. The something else is a community in which the lineaments of a rational life are etched in a relatively intractable material. Unless that task is passionately pursued, and with some measure of success, the university is likely to become special advocate now for this importunate cause and later for that, and in the alternation more determined by rhetoricians than by philosophers if one may invoke a classically invidious distinction.

This is but to frame anew the constitutive paradox of the university. It summons us to learn the arts and benefits of the reflective life before we try to change the world, even while we seem to hear the world crying, " Change me before it is too late! "

It is not to be doubted, however, that the rational life has been given quite a beating, a most unholy thumping in fact, by learned and prophetic spirits. True, most of these seers and savants have kept small candles burning at the feet of the goddess Reason. The most dogged behaviorist is still in favor of persuading his critic rather than of modifying the unbeliever's " mind " with drugs, electrical charges, surgery, or bullets. As a scientist he propounds a theory that is capable of being understood by a competent person. He is in favor of advancing understanding. He is a protagonist of knowledge. He is a true believer in the sovereignty of truth. He knows that the university exists to further the pursuit of truth by the proper cultivation of the powers of reason.

Fortunately we do not need to suppose that these articles of faith are abhorrent to the generality of students. To many of them, but not to them alone, dedication to the cultivation of reason sounds rather stuffy as causes and slogans go. But conscious dedication to the cause of Unreason is surely as absurd as its antithesis is stuffy. We should hope that there was agreement, broad and clear, on this. Suppose, however, that absurdity is hypostatized and from that process emerges as the Absurd, and summons the shade of Camus to hallow it. Then choices other than the cultivation of reason begin to multiply, and the temple of the university is in a fair way to become a pantheon. Therein heroes give way to antiheroes. The Knight of Reason, once clad in shining armor, skulks in the shadows, a fustian creature. Even Hume, with his wonderful slogan, " Reason is and ought to be the slave of the passions," belongs to the party of the Establishment — no revolutionary, he. Hume and Hollywood are not in perfect agreement on the meaning of " passion," but neither are many students and Hollywood. Passion has become a proper synonym for commitment. Commitment is wholehearted dedication to the party of high principle in the scorching crises in American life. Away then with detachment! Detachment is the choice of the coward, the cynic, and the idle observer of tragic encounter.

Thus we must cope with the spreading conviction that ethical commitment, if it be really ethical, demands open and relentless conflict with the power structure. The masters of the power structure claim to have reasonableness on their side. Either they lie, or Reason is a whore. In either case it is not profitable to waste time in high-level debate. The crisis demands action rather than protracted inquiry, and commitment rather than reflection. How then can we legitimately avoid thinking of the university as a reservoir of moral passion rather than as an asylum for the life of ordered reflection?

Here is a disagreement reaching into the heart of the university. It promises radically to modify the idea of the university. We seem to be moving under irresistible pressure toward the view that the highest aim of the university is to make people better than they would otherwise have been, and toward the belief that " better " means a greater and purer readiness to be engaged on the right side of the great conflicts in which life and liberty, rather than happiness and success, are at stake.

These things are not yet certain. They are questions and they do not yet elicit automatic affirmatives. But they do point up the fact that the university has become a unique cockpit of the value conflicts raging in American society. We cannot represent the university as being above the battle. The university man cannot represent himself as being primarily the philosophic diagnostician of the ills of society. It would surely be a mistake to suppose that this disagreement over the idea of the university is a providential opportunity for making traditional Christian perspectives once more fully at home in the center of the university. These perspectives are in fact commonly spurned by rationalists and nonrationalists, and by the protagonists of detachment and the prophets of engagement. To people of all these parties, " Christian perspectives " smacks of antique loyalties long since transcended by enlightened and ethically sensitive men. So whoever would persist in injecting the Christian thing into the cockpit of the university must already have swept or burned away everything metaphysically offensive in it and left only an open and shining face of ethical passion.

What then could be more outlandishly quixotic, indeed more outrageously backworldly, than to propose that the cockpit of the university become again the arena of explicit premeditated theological argument in which Christian perspectives, as metaphysical as the very devil, must take their chances, and ask no more of predisposition or precommitment than the aforementioned devil or, come to think of it, rather less?

That is what I propose. But before this is done, frontally and in cold blood, there are anterior matters to which some attention ought to be paid. One of these is particularly interesting. It is the notion, to which some theologians have lent considerable persuasiveness, that we are already on the premises of religion, or at any rate of religiousness, when we find ourselves making absolute commitments. Be that as it may. We have to note that to speak of commitments as absolute is to suggest that some commitments are or might be tentative and relative. This suggestion again stirs dusty memories of those debates (O bright college years) in which the claims of reason were read as incompatible with absolute commitments, and the philosopher emerged — often enough in response to his own invocation — as the one who reserved an essential something of his own being in reserving judgment upon all claims on his capacity for loyalty and for accepting loyalties. Whoever could not deduce from this that the man of faith was unwitting kinsman of blind and ferocious fanatics was obviously retarded or perverse.

Thus the immediate objective is a look at absolute commitment. Things badly need sorting out in this area.

II

Faith as a religious phenomenon can plausibly be represented as absolute devotion to some being or some value. Christian faith can therefore be construed as absolute devotion to that strangest of all beings, God. Unless the strangeness of that object of devotion can be philosophically (that is, rationally) dissolved, Christian theology remains as an affront — no less offensive for being so ancient — to the rational idea of the university. It leaves something beyond the reach of the all-searching critical spirit. Some theologians are willing accomplices in that dissolution. They may hope that their contribution to that will restore theology to academic respectability. I do not intend here to argue the merits of that posture. For the moment the question is what to make of " absolute devotion." I suggest that we think of it as unreserved commitment. " Unreserved " is a quality of decision not to be confused with the quantitative term " total." When I drive out of the sylvan quiet of my street into the traffic on a main artery I am making a total commitment. My life, career, family loves and responsibilities, political loyalties, everything is put in jeopardy; I am entrusting the whole works to my driving skills and to the luck of the draw of other drivers I shall encounter. Of course I expect to withdraw from that chancy affair without making in so doing a significant change either in myself or in the lives of the other gamblers on the road. (I am not assuming or arguing the defects of the famous doctrine of internal relations at this point. Commonsensically I am the same person who could have turned at Santa Fe Street rather than at Swarthmore. If I had turned at Santa Fe, my " real being " would not have been significantly modified. A few minutes later than usual I should have turned up as pretty much the same being who usually remembers the street on which he lives. Some great philosophers doubt this. They want Reality to be in on every trick and turn.)

But when I say to another person, " I will be faithful to you forever," or when I say to God, " I will obey you rather than man," many of my interests are at best on the perimeters of such commitments, and surely others lie quite beyond them. My bridge game, for instance, is not likely to be affected. If my faith should be mistaken, one way or another, I might go right on playing bridge. In fact, I might then go at bridge with great relief. So if my wife should say, " You promised to give up bridge to cling to me only," it would be reasonable to suppose that either she or I had confused unreserved commitment with a *quid pro quo* deal of some sort. Confusions like this are common. Their frequency does not generate nobility for them.

Absolute devotion in the sense of unreserved commitment expresses the vital center of one's life. There is nothing to prevent ventures of such magnitude from failing; and fail they do. When that happens one's life may go on, but it goes on as habit, as a bundle of reflexes. The point of it has been blunted or lost, and the world has become just one damned thing after another.

Here we pause to pay our respects to paradoxical features of the relations of total and unreserved commitments. Consider, for example, the fact that we normally do not expect total commitments in the everyday world to make much of a difference, and yet they are life-and-death decisions, or may well prove to be. They rarely feel like that. Crossing the street does not seem to be that important, and generally it is not really important at all. Nonetheless lives are lost in idle pursuit of transient pleasures. I cross the street to get a better look at the woman walking on that side and I am struck down in the prime of life and curiosity. I go for a pleasant ride on Sunday afternoon in the country, and suddenly there is going to be no Monday for me.

What we call the everyday world is in fact a curious fabric of total commitments extracted or solicited from us all. But the oddity of the fabric generally eludes our attention and understanding. When we are compelled to think about it we often reach for the cold comfort of Fate: his car and mine were programmed to meet head on that lovely spring Sunday. A few minutes more with *The Times* or a few minutes less, and all would have been well. But it was not to be that the salvific time would be allotted.

Unreserved commitment is a decision for one life rather than for another. It is momentous but it is not fateful. This means that unreserved commitments are not appropriately represented as effects flowing from inscrutable cosmic decrees. Indeed, we might justifiably reserve " decision " to signify the blend of freedom and necessity that confronts us as unreserved commitment. And if we proceed thence to construe " faith " as a form of unreserved commitment, we ought to see more clearly than ever why confusions of faith and fate with each other produce such grotesque distortions of man's spirit.

An unreserved commitment may require a total expenditure of oneself. I may be called upon to die for what I wholly love. To withdraw or even to qualify that love because of that risk would argue excellently that I loved myself more than the avowed other. Surely the risks are there. Love and faith can lead one into the valley of the shadow of death well ahead of the time when any inclination or any failure of nature would do so. The " tragic sense " is inflamed by our contemplating the possibility, realized countless times in history, that love and faith even unto

32

death may be lavished upon unworthy and unreal objects. Such waste gratifies the tragic sense but it offends moralistic sentiments and a reality principle. The latter is by far the greater offense. Really to be human demands unreserved commitment to actual persons rather than to abstractions and fantasies. Love may indeed be wasted upon the unlovable. Faith may indeed be betrayed. These are tragic events, whenever and to whomever they happen. But the criterion informing that judgment is a primitive apprehension of reality antecedent to the tragic sense. An indestructible cliché contains this primordial knowing: " Better to have loved and lost than never to have loved at all." Better than the life upon which no real love has been expended.

III

The university does not exist to be a secondary parent, teaching its young how to love and how to be faithful, on the assumption — in fact, reasonable enough — that these indispensable capacities in its young have not yet been activated. Naturally the university offers guidance, and more and more of it. It is not easy to become a person, and the university itself is threatening to become an excessively difficult context for this all-important transaction. Perhaps this may help to account for the multiplication of guidance facilities in the university. On the other hand, I suppose that a classical assumption still operates in the sense of responsibility to be a wise guide to the young. I mean the assumption that becoming a person requires the development of the powers of reason. One must learn to discriminate, to check and recheck, to think out implications, and to envisage consequences. In a word, and an ancient one at that, one must learn "to test all things and hold fast to that which is good."

Such a delineation of the classical assumption in the role of the university as a guide to the perplexed gives the cognitive enterprise of the university a secondary rank. In the end, or before it, we may need to revise the rankings. Here we are trying to press the critical function as far as possible into the idea of the university. The intent is to test a prevalent notion about the university, namely, that the university as such is the paradigmatic disinterested critic of all " concerns ": all loves and all faiths.

Such a notion of the university does not exclude the possibility of a " love divine, all loves excelling " at the heart of the Establishment. It does make this all-compelling love a love of the rational good. And it invites the translation of the rational good into the good of exercising the powers of criticism upon everything else.

So if we want to test this idea of the university, we may properly begin it by looking at criticism itself. What is this thing of the mind that it should be King of Hearts in the life of the university, whether or not it is now in bad odor or even languishing in exile vile?

The preternaturally clever schoolboy knows that " criticism " is roughly synonymous with " evaluation," " judging," " testing," etc., which is to say that to criticize something is to weigh it and thereafter to judge it. To judge it is to grasp the essentials of the thing and thereafter to set forth what it is in respect to its being and its value.

Thus the rational life is that one in which appearances and plausibilities are sagaciously and relentlessly tested, in the hope that the realities will be veraciously disclosed in this process. Thereafter what is worthy of acceptance and commendation will be accepted and commended. Thus the rational life stands out against the life of spontaneous enjoyment either of weal or woe, bane or blessing. And it also stands out against abstract understanding of what is and what is good. The rational life is one in which the right things are rightly enjoyed.

God knows, and we are entitled to suspect, that the demands of rationality so conceived are seldom realized in any earthly institution. This sad fact does not invalidate the claims of the ideal. Indeed we ought to honor no effort to invalidate that ideal. Our goal is more modest and more sane: To discern the actual structures generated and preserved by pursuit of the ideal. This modest undertaking rests on the assumption that devotion to an ideal is perforce expressed as loyalty to actual structures of human life. This loyalty may be far from wholehearted or unreserved but it is a prerequisite for the critical endeavor projected here.

IV

Criticism is a tool for the refinement of human possibilities. This operation is directed upon concrete expressions of human powers. So the critic comes to light in a situation he did not devise. Many of the features of this situation, moreover, are impervious to any critical attack he might dream of making upon them. What I have in mind here are not the massive institutions upon which theologians in the modern mood have fit the notion of original sin. We cannot reasonably deny that these massive institutions change slowly, or that changes in them rarely flow from reason. But here I am thinking of those features or elements of the given world which a critic needs for his trade. These are not the subject matter of criticism but are, instead, its aims and criteria. The critic cannot accept these elements provisionally. He can accept them contingently, but this contingency is a quality of a human decision, a quality manifested in all human decisions. So understood, contingency pertains to human act rather than to an object with which action deals. And thus again freedom and necessity are visible in the actual fabric of human life, whatever metaphysical prepossessions and systems may induce us to accept or to deny.

At the moment theologians rather than metaphysicians are likely to discover something uncommonly meaty in this situation. For now the critic emerges as a man of faith: he has faith in the instruments and the benefits of the critical process. And the person who says, " Let intelligence prevail! " is advertising the supremacy of his god.

Perhaps there is something admirable in this theological generosity in so distributing the virtue — or is it the necessity? — of faith. If so, it may be meanspirited to file a demurrer, but the risk must be run. The person who says, " Let intelligence prevail! " is so far simply one who has large confidence in his own powers of reason, in his own intelligence. This confidence may turn out to be misplaced, but we cannot predict that. If this turns out to be so, the Christian believer does not have in that a very good reason for rejoicing, even if he tries to cash it out as the just reward of pride. Moreover, a person convinced of the eminence of intelligence and prepared to recommend it unreservedly to others had better have learned its value from his own exercise of it, whether or not the results have been world-shaking. Otherwise he simply has it on hearsay that intelligence is a good thing. He believes it on authority or instinct (authority being a kind of social instinct) , whereas others, whom apparently he admires or even envies, have good reason for believing it.

But of course it may well be the case that some people do look up to intelligence as to a grand cause and a god above all others. This hardly obscures the fact that faith in intelligence is a poor candidate for unreserved commitment. For suppose that a true believer in intelligence admits that he is really prepared to follow and to obey it only so far as it proves reliable. Is he not admitting that his dependency upon it is, after all, relative — that is conditional — rather than absolute? Or is he? We are nonplussed to divine what faculty one would use to detect and describe the point at which intelligence had let one down if the same were **not** some arm of intelligence.

So a confession of conditional dependence upon **intelli-**

gence would seem to be quite like the more colorful confession of the Old Testament prophet who asks, " Shall not
the Judge of all the earth do right? " The prophet is hardly
claiming a knowledge of right independent of the word of
God. He is claiming the right of personal application of
the right disclosed by the word of God. Since God has in
fact disclosed the right to him, he must use it as the foundation and the criterion for appraising everything claiming
divine authority. Having made an unreserved commitment
to this same God, and being in that a man of faith, he does
not expect or suppose that the object of this commitment
will let him down, though he may find much to wonder at
in the ways his God tests the measure and quality of his
faith.

Something at once protests that viewing intelligence as a
god is very different from the faith of the prophet. But what
is the difference in the cases? A simple, straightforward answer comes immediately to mind. What way do we have of
knowing whether or when intelligence has let us down?
How can the critic of any human performance get on with
his work if he must suppose that intelligence has ever been
or will ever be fickle, to say nothing of traitorous? If he
supposed that his judgments would dissolve into intuitions,
he would not be able to marshal any hard evidence to support his intuitions. We generally think poorly of such critics. So great is our common need to use intelligence as an
indispensable instrument for understanding and furthering
any essential human concern that we cannot conceive —
though we can indeed imagine — being actually betrayed
by this instrument. We may use it badly, but there we betray ourselves rather than anything properly divine.

The experience expressed as being under the wrath of
God is a very different case. This is the sense of having betrayed a trust on which pivots all that is meaningful in
life and in the world. Faith in God establishes a framework and a structure of relationships within which one

37

must use one's best judgment in working out and in appraising policies. So understood, faith is not an instrument to be used. The instrumental relationship presupposes a framework within which the exercise of intelligence normally is self-reduced to the acquisition and exercise of technical competence.

Thus if God were really to fail us, rather than our failing him, no life-style (no range and mode of execution of commitments) could claim eminence. Even the choice of life over death would descend to the determination of instinct, which, if Freud be right, is a slender and ambiguous reed at best.

I do not intend that the contrast between commitment to intelligence and faith in God should have any other point or merit than this: The elevation of an instrumentality of human life to the status of divinity yields singularly unhappy results, whether the instrumentality is intelligence itself or faith itself. Accordingly, theologians of every stripe have heavy stakes in trying to represent faith as the work of God himself. The motive is right, whatever we make of any given performance.

What, then, persists in interpreting unreserved commitment as a dire threat to the refinement of critical powers as the proper end of the university? Principally a hardy utopianism concerning the freedom of the intellect. So belief in central elements of traditional Christianity is often represented as a commitment bad enough in an individual but vastly more threatening to the free flow of criticism when it carries institutional endorsement.

Accordingly the "free university" has come to mean an institution that as such endorses no belief except belief in the cultivation of those critical powers which are indispensable to the extension of knowledge and to the sound governance of human affairs. How then can we reasonably avoid the inference that " Christian " and " free " cannot both qualify " university "? Is it sufficient, or even fair, to counterattack this view of the university by accusing it of being an ahistorical utopianism?

The matter is too weighty to be settled by invocational slogans of any party. At the least it calls for further reflection on criticism itself.

V

Criticism is an evaluative activity. Its relationship to the cognitive enterprise is complex. I consider here only two aspects of this complexity: (1) the way in which criticism draws upon reflection for analytical rather than for world-exploratory purposes and (2) the concentration of criticism upon those creations in which the distinctiveness of human life is exhibited.

1. Criticism engages us in a unique grappling with what purports to be fact and with what purports to be value. When we engage in criticism we are analyzing the results of human cognitive and creative activities. This is not the same as conducting an exploration into the nature of things. A critic may be influenced by his hunches and dogmas about the nature of things. But ideally his reflective powers are trained upon such precommitments for cautionary purposes primarily. " Be on guard against your own a priori fiats. They might be sound; but sound or not, they are likely to emit interference signals when you interpret what man has wrought." Something like that is the counsel of the critic to himself relative to hunches and dogmas about the nature of things.

How, then, does criticism really differ from the cognitive enterprise? As products of the age of science we can scarcely doubt that science has long since become the personal name for the realm of knowledge. Nor can we doubt that the scientist is committed in principle to a rigorous systematic testing of truth-claims that create strains in the established knowledge system, which is his science at any given moment.

We must be wary of privileged and *ad hoc* distinctions,

but our wariness must not suppress chance-taking. The chance I have in mind is this one: The function (indeed the obligation) of the critic is not to challenge the scientist on the scientist's own ground. To do that effectively he would need to be scientist rather than critic. He comes into his own as critic when he asks some such question as, " All right, here is the knowledge system. Now what is its *human* value? "

This is not like asking, " What are the presuppositions of that knowledge system? " That may be a very important question. It ought not to be confused with the critical question, even though this confusion is all but inevitable. It is in fact a philosophical habit people claimed to have acquired from studying and believing Kant. I do not know that the habit can be broken — criticism may be precondemned to Kantian imprisonment — but the risk is well worth taking.

So we say again that the critic probes a knowledge system for a range of inferences rather than for a submerged mass of presuppositions. The critic tests a knowledge system for its inferences affecting the human condition. For this purpose his equipment cannot be limited to philosophically systematic understandings of " inference." Moreover, the human condition for which the critic holds a watching brief is not a set of abstractions or a set of empirical generalizations. It is human life in this time and this space. It is this history, the history of the critic's people, and not history in general.

This focus upon and this obligation to the concrete, the particular, the bounded, and the provincial, generates a paradox in the critic. Perhaps we shall be able to see this more clearly by again contrasting the critic with the scientist, the latter being the paradigmatic cognizer in our culture.

The scientist claims membership in an international intellectual society chartered for the discovery and the free promulgation of knowledge for its own sake. If that society had a heraldic device, it would have emblazoned on it, " Truth is strong and shall prevail! " Prevail not only over ignorance but also over arbitrary restrictions and violent repressions springing from "dominations and principalities." It is important to add this lest we suppose that the scientific community, of which the university is a local chapter, has to contend only with an ideal enemy, namely ignorance, rather than with political regimes dedicated to power rather than to truth.

But surely the critic (I am of course dealing with ideal types at the moment) is entitled to believe that he too is a member of an international intellectual society? I think not, no matter how many international congresses of his pet learned society he may manage to attend at the expense of his university. The critic may hope that his critical performance will commend itself to the right-thinking as a rational act, but his subject is a human creation whose roots go down into a particular culture. He is not chartered to find in that creation something eternally meaningful. Of course he may believe that this creation has something in it for everybody in all times and places. But before he can properly go about to show that, he must come to grips with it just as it is, a creation whose ostensive value is derived from a particular set of historicocultural perimeters. Even if he invokes truth, beauty, and goodness as such, he does so only to hint at the most comprehensive demands of ideality. True, proper reflection upon this creation may show that its real value, as distinguished from its ostensive value, approaches universality asymptotically. But as a product of criticism, this requires criticism. Otherwise the claim to universality may be cultural imperialism in disguise. Here the scientist seems to occupy an enviable position. So long as he sticks to his science, the threat of his performance becoming cultural imperialism is very remote. As a social phenomenon science honors no provincial masters. Its methods

41

and its results do not presuppose the cultural superiority of any who master them and even less the ethical superiority.

Perhaps again at this point we should be reminded that we are so far dealing with ideal types. In fact, severe crises in the life of his nation may quickly drive the scientist to an anguished engagement with the " dominations and principalities." He may feel morally bound to assist in the conversion of his science into weapons of prodigious destructiveness. Thereafter he may claim that his physics transcends the boundaries of the nation, but he certainly does not transcend them. He can but hope that the use of his science in the interest of national security — or, for that matter, his refusal to permit its use — will be justified in the end. In the end, not by the end. About the end judgment he can only have hopes. About that his science as such gives him neither aid nor comfort.

The critic is not committed or condemned to any such eschatological justification. He holds a watching brief in behalf of the human. As critic he has no knowledge system that can be converted into weaponry, either physical or psychological. But he has a responsibility as unenviable as that of the scientist, and that is to test the creations of his civilization for their humanity. " Humanity " is not quite the same as " humaneness." The critic is set to look for what in a human creation reveals or belies the essentially human. But to find *that,* he had better go down rather than out. If there is anything of universal import in his subjects, it will be buried in a dense thicket of provinciality. If provinciality offends him to the point of revulsion, he may never catch the scent of the universal if indeed the scent is there. And if it is there, rooted firmly in a provincial matrix, to disclose it he will need other instruments than the exquisitely precise but very limited tools of technical logic. If he advertises " a science of interpretation," he will need to make it very clear that its articulations are certainly not those of linear inference. And this is scarcely more than to say that criticism is more like an art than it is like a science.

2. The inclusive aim of criticism is to enhance appreciation of a given range of expressions of human creativity. Specific concrete achievements are the immediate objects of this criticism. The critic hopes to uncover with his craft the real value of a human creation. If there is a presupposition here, it is the conviction that appreciation of a creation commonly needs refinement. Enjoyment of creativity and of its products can benefit from ordered reflection. " Ordered reflection " unfortunately can degenerate into readiness to swap native unreasoned prejudice for the more plausible prejudices of the critic. This is at once a corruption of criticism and an exploitation of the student. Ideally criticism is activity calculated to enhance appreciation of what is really there in a human creation.

What, then, is appreciation? To appreciate something is to apprehend its actual value. Thereafter one may properly proceed to embrace it as good or to reject it as bad.

To put it thus is to suggest a kind of theological assumption: A kind of original sin is embedded in culture, and this is a natural propensity for creating and enjoying the fraudulent. It would be a more modest claim to have discovered a native readiness to substitute the plausible for the true, the ostensive for the real. Why else is criticism necessary? Why is it necessary to put all human creations to the test? Why else does the critic presume to interfere with natural processes and with the results of spontaneous expression and unreflective enjoyment?

The arrogance of theological presumption is considerably reduced by this answer: All human drives and sensibilities require structuring. Once this structure (" civilization ") is achieved and has been grafted into the individual, he may learn that it has a place for spontaneous expression and unreflective enjoyment. But he may also discover that this place is defined by visible perimeters and that it is regulated by powerful sanctions. If he thinks further about these things, he may discover that artists and other moralists who espouse the " natural " have highly stylized rhetorics in which they make their case.

So there is nothing unusually promising for theology in the homely truth that to exist as a human being means accepting inwardly as well as outwardly a particular culturation. One need not accept that system as final or supreme. Man is the talking animal. One must learn a specific language because there is no language in general. But one may discover that another language, although equally specific and historically conditioned (whatever that may mean) has superior expressive resources. Man is also a religious animal. One cannot be religious in general. One must start by being religious in a particular way, but theologians themselves are handy illustrations of the equally inescapable fact that one need not stop with what one has started. So one may go on to another religion. The critical point about all such progressions from the given to the presumptively more excellent is whether they are made reflectively and responsibly. Or are they made by the pressure of something like a herd instinct?

Thus the critic is expected to discharge a large and serious service, namely, to teach his contemporaries how to understand the human creations with which they are surrounded. He is, moreover, called upon to do this in a way that does not obscure the lineaments of the human condition as such. This is to say that his appraisals ought not to exhibit or inspire an uncritical preference for the familiar and native expressions of his own society. At the same time, the critic ought not to allow his contemporaries to fall into an easy disdain for the familiar and native simply because it is that. So if a critic tells us that Modigliani was profoundly influenced by the primitive art of Africa, we ought to be alarmed or even outraged if he tells us that Modigliani is therefore to be rejected. The critic ought not to use a term such as " primitivist " unless he has taken every reasonable caution against its being understood as an accusation. Primitive art is higly stylized indeed. But given some of the predispositions of American culture, the uncorrected and uncriticized word " primitive " smacks and is supposed to smack of subhuman life mysteriously continued after the beginning of high and holy history. It may still be the case that no amount of instruction will modify one's appreciation for the primitive. But it is not the business of the critic to multiply the number of persons who enjoy Modigliani. It is the business of the critic to sharpen and to deepen appreciation for what is there no matter what its origins or its congruence with natural preferences. This is hard work. Some human creations cannot be easily understood. A poet, for example, may produce things that are cryptic, threatening, or scholarly, or all of them at once. So one finds oneself asking, " If I must work so hard to understand a *poem,* can it be worth the effort? " That question cannot be answered decisively in advance of the effort. Too, mass culture puts a heavy premium on the things that can be easily assimilated and that can confirm the value preferences of such a culture. Here again one can become obsessed with the importance of distinguishing oneself from the masses, to the point where the unintelligibility, or better yet the sheer nastiness, of a work of art is overpriced simply because it drives off the multitudes. Such attitudes are at least as difficult to get at critically as the natural preferences of the untutored.

The work of refining sensibility calls for singular combinations of singular gifts. Much in the life of the university bears this out but nothing more clearly than the profound reluctance of graduate schools to instruct their students in the art of teaching. That, apparently, is not one of the liberal arts. It is not a science, either, even though learning and communication are matters into which psychology is pushing many research salients.

Theology and the Church in the University

It would be wrong to suggest that the university has been laggard in producing rationalizations for this situation. Of these none is more common than the solemn asseveration that the university is committed to teaching people how to think rather than what to believe and otherwise appreciate. Large and powerful sectors of the university do not even give lip service to this sentiment. I mean particularly the scientific sector. The reason is clear. There men believe that the cognitive enterprise has achieved its greatest triumphs in the history of mankind. So there criticism is a recessive feature of the business. Science in the modern world is not designed to enhance man's appreciation of nature. The metaphysical-mystical element in cognition, that is, the penetration of the secrets of reality, is dwarfed by the drive for power. " Science " and " technology " have become synonymous in the popular understanding of science. This view of science is frequently corroborated by vigorous antimetaphysical expostulations of scientists. Here scientists expose a soft flank to philosophical attack. Many scientists are insufficiently critical about their own assumptions. When these assumptions seem to be there as formidable submerged masses of presuppositions, philosophers may feel there is nothing for it but to launch the enterprise of dredging for presuppositions. Theologians stand on the shore ready to christen whatever is thereby disclosed as " faith." But for their own part, scientists do not act as though they had learned anything from this game that they need in order to get on with their own game.

We may then ask, What is the real point of the philosopher's game? Apart, that is, from dredging for presuppositions. We are not likely to be convinced that the university exists as a set of exercises in logic. The " how to think," which is the critical aim, is a kind of concrete or material evaluation of the human world. This does not call for an enormous expansion of the ranks of professional critics. It does require the most painstaking attention to ways in which the powers of criticism may be developed, and this on the grand Socratic principle that " the unexamined life is not worth living." Should we conclude that reflection creates values? Not yet, certainly, if at all or ever. (Only Aristotle's God could get everything from thinking about thinking; and only he, so far as he did not design to do so.) Some values are enhanced by reflection. Some values are discoverable only by reflection, one of those being the benefits of reflection itself. But we ought not to sit by dumbly when the arts of criticism are confused with creativity. Criticism presupposes the products of creativity.

Perhaps we have here again stumbled upon a kind of original sin. I mean what seems to be an innate propensity of civilization eventually to cheapen its own values. Given this dismal history, this melancholy propensity, critical powers must be quickened in order to distinguish the valid from the meretricious, the real article from the debased imitation. (The distinction between the valid and invalid is itself likely to be obscured or even corrupted by its being confused with the distinction between the traditional and the novel.) Why does every civilization eventually debase its currency, both monetary and cultural? Why does the meretricious capture the multitudes? Perhaps creativity demands too much and is too poorly rewarded. Perhaps the creative spirits are already shaping the world of tomorrow before the rest of us have got used to the present world.

In the university, there is an acute awareness of the debased coinage enjoying wide currency in contemporary culture. Meretricious things are not only popular. They are climbing the heights of power, glory, and honor. So we have a correspondingly heavy premium put on criticism as a check against this raging tide. But the premium put upon criticism is also construed as a down payment upon something more than criticism can yield. The great desideratum is a humane order of values. We sense, rather than clearly know, that a structure of belief at once adequately rational

47

and fully supportive of a humane order of values, is at least equally important. But many in the university suppose that such marvelous things can be generated out of the depths of the critical spirit, provided that it be sufficiently critical. Many suppose that could we but give undivided and undistracted attention to learning how to think, we should have settled by that what to believe and for what to hope. Others suppose that these issues can be adjudicated by something like the technical developments of human reason involved in the scientific pursuit of knowledge. Science teaches us how to find out what is the case. Why do people, otherwise apparently intelligent, persist in believing that the life of reflection must have other resources and not just other problems? That is a question we must ponder.

VI

It has become popular dogma that a university provides the optimum context for the development of the critical spirit when it is institutionally indifferent to religious options. The popularity of this sentiment is not a criterion of merit. And it can hardly stifle questions, two of which come immediately to mind. The first is whether religious indifferentism as university policy makes the historical development of a given university irrelevant to the determination of its present policies. A second question is whether or not commitments of the kind outlined above really constitute a threat to the critical autonomy of any member of the university. I should like to comment briefly on these issues.

Legal considerations aside, I do not believe that the historical development of a university is automatically irrelevant to its present and future life no matter how dense the air is with the dust and smoke of rapid and violent social change. This is not to recommend nonchalance in the face of social disintegration and (hopefully) renewal. There is, nonetheless, some merit in espousing an initial skepticism about a presumptively universal ideal of what the good university is. Human life is of course vulnerable to pressure from the realm of ideality, and the people of the university are not entirely protected against such pressure. But is it too close to cynicism, rather than to honest skepticism, to suggest that the university is characteristically much more prone to respond to the demands of contemporary society than to solicitations emanating from ideality? Society needs leaders of such and such capabilities, and it needs myrmidons to follow these leaders. Beyond these needs loom (or lurk) uncharted realms of the world luring the cognitive powers to enter them, for better and worse. But the university does not yet have a monopoly upon cognition. We may moreover reasonably wonder whether the university is so committed to the cognitive enterprise that its service function has become secondary. I do not at all mean that "knowledge" and "service" are mutually incompatible ideals. Yet it is the case, I think, that the pressures of society upon the university are relentlessly instrumentalistic. "Knowledge" thus becomes "knowledge of how to . . ."; and knowledge of being seems an absurd pursuit both to plain citizens and to top-heavy philosophers.

Moreover, even the grand solicitations of truth are variously heard and variously responded to. History, quite as much as temperament, is a great source of this variety. Each of us pursues truth, and resists it, from an individual and often idiosyncratic matrix. So also for universities. Distinctiveness of tradition and determination to honor it by incorporating its best features into ongoing life do not of themselves argue worship of idols.

Secondly, I do not believe that the persistence of a religious tradition of itself is in any way a threat to the critical autonomy of the university or to any of its personnel. Obviously, much depends upon the kind of religious tradition involved and upon the way in which its values are represented and recommended. A considerable part of the bur-

49

den of this essay is to make distinctions in the ways in which commitment to religious tradition functions and ought to function in a university. At this point I want to stress the fact (for I take it to be a fact) that the importance of religious options can hardly be seriously displayed, to say nothing of being communicated, by persons to whom religious commitment is foreign.

By " religious options " I mean the religious communities whose history is intertwined with the history of Western culture rather than life-attitudes worked out on one's own. Thus I do not suppose that " religious options " is some way of being privately religious, or some way of being religious independently of a historicoreligious community. No doubt being privately religious accords well with much else that has been called the privatization of contemporary life but it accords ill with religion and not at all with the Christian faith. As for life-attitude, the supposition that it is the heart of religion is a peculiarly academic superstition.

Accordingly, to speak seriously of the importance of being religious is to allow for a case being made for a particular concrete religious commitment. Religion is not taken seriously when it is blandly supposed that one cannot help being religious. People can avoid being virtuous, and it is not the business of the moralist to convince them that they really cannot avoid it. So also people can avoid being religious, and it is not the business of the theologian to convince them that this is an illusion. Students may be edified by hearing enlightened and urbane professors assure them that religion is or has been a vital part of the human story. Surely they ought to be impressed by the rich documentation for this claim gathered from contemporary (I hesitate to say modern) Mississippi as well as from ancient Mesopotamia. But a considerable number of these same students have never seen anybody *being* religious — being, that is, unfeignedly and unselfconsciously religious. Of these a fair number are ready to assess religious demands and claims in the abstract, that is, by the application of explicitly — and often militantly — nonreligious principles, philosophical or scientific. Those who do know something about religious life at first hand and have been practicing religious people may well have come to doubt that the religion *they* know can survive the application of rigorous criticism to it. Thus the desperate attempts to preserve familial piety from any exposure to harsh criticism. Such attempts do not lose their pathos for being corporate rather than private. Indeed, one of the most depressing spectacles a campus can offer is that of a group of religious people trying to protect a sense of corporate identity and importance against the inroads of what passes locally as enlightenment. We can hardly doubt that many a hardy and cheerful campus atheist, upon seeing this spectacle, murmurs to himself, " There, but for the grace of God, go I! " and in pity and embarrassment passes by on the other side of the road.

So many come to believe, and are actually led to believe, that religious commitments are far more likely to wither in the bright sun of criticism than almost any other kind of commitment or interest. Other commitments are encouraged, rather than merely permitted, to grow from innocence into (or at least toward) sophistication and depth. For many students, as for many of their mentors, the analogous movement in religion is from having one to having none.

A fair part of the explanation of this odd situation lies in the persistence of Comtian and Freudian dogmas about religion. Whatever the explanation, the situation is an odd one. Respecting other elements of the spiritual life, the college rarely hesitates to commend as well as to criticize. Art, in all or much of her diversity, is pursued as well as interpreted. Despite the snide distinction between philosophers

51

Theology and the Church in the University

and professors of philosophy, the college endorses the philosophic spirit even when the local philosophers have fore-
closed on all the traditional problems of philosophy. But
nowadays one comes upon even church-related colleges
where an ancient and honorable tradition is civilly saluted
in the college catalog and the practice of religion is exhausted by thin exercises from which Catholics and Jews
are excused for conscience's sake, since to require their at-
tendance would be a clear denial of their religious liberty.
And all kinds of people promptly and passionately join the
chorus hollering " Foul! " when one observes, even in the
most amicable vein, that such a college is still a voluntary
society, at least at the point of admission, and that a Catholic or a Jew ought to think twice before jeopardizing his
spiritual health, if not his immortal soul, by signing on for
a tour of duty in a Methodist school.

Not that higher-level and more meaningful objections are
lacking. Far from it. Consider this one. How can a college
pretend to be a church? It is one thing for a sociologist to
discourse about religious cults and codes. It would be quite
another if he opened each of his class sessions with a celebration of the Lord's Supper. To be sure, much of college
life is cultic. The faculty is hierarchical in structure, and
some of its members are hieratic in posture and pronounce-
ment. But it is fair to say that all such formations and
processes are nontheological, and hardly any claims Revelation as its ground and warrant.

The fact that a college adopts a churchly role whether or
not the college is halfhearted in that role is a more serious
problem than another one encountered at least as frequently, viz., that the kind of criticism the college can do
best requires that kind of objectivity called neutrality. I
simply do not believe it to be so that the people who have
thought most productively about religion are the people
who have known nothing in themselves of its practice. One

might of course come forward out of religious nonbeing with a novel and exciting theory about religion. But how would such a one know what the theory was good for? How would such a one go about assaying religious testimony? Nothing in the world prevents a man from giving a non-religious explanation of religious testimony. Nothing in the world requires the religious person to give any religious substance to such an explanation. Scientific explanations of art do not generate any insight into the meaning of art, to say nothing of scientific explanations of the artist. We cannot say less of scientific theories of religion or of any particular religion.

No real mystery confronts us in this situation. Religious behavior presumably is no less open to general principles and patterns of explanation than any other kind of behavior. But religious testimony is also explanation. In his testimony the religious man is also giving an account of things, and these are commonly things of the greatest magnitude. This holds for pietism as well as for other modes of the religious life, for the pietist is doing more than telling us about the ineffable interiority of his being. He sings the praises of the blessed Christ, the same being much more real, in his account, than the postman, the undertaker, and the mitered bishop. Like all other religious, the pietist is sure he knows the shape and savor of the ultimately real and the wholly good. We may be offended or amused by his language and outraged by his claim to be especially favored by God, but if we want really to damage or, more modestly, to balance his testimony, we will have to offer some testimony of our own. It is not enough for us to presume that reality has already given the lie to his account, as though there were a fund of metaphysical certainties upon which we can write more adequate drafts.

The consensus of a university does often seem to run merrily toward such presumption. There are things which all up-to-date people know to be true. These truths are no longer mere beliefs; they are like the gold of Fort Knox: to deny its existence is the silliest of all skepticisms because it is the least practical, and the skeptic who becomes impractical has lost his justification.

If criticism is a good thing, we might well conclude that it is good for the university as a whole and as such. Thus it is not enough for us to imagine or presume that a given religious testimony is wrong. We must somehow seek to show that it is wrong. The issue, accordingly, is not only the conflict of metaphysical beliefs with one another. It is also the matching of metaphysical arguments.

VII

Christian commitment in the university does not always create the context most favorable for metaphysical argument. When the church goes into the college business it is sometimes guilty of great shortcomings, of which none is more conspicuous or more grievous than reluctance to press for an open airing of the prime metaphysical issues in which the stake of the nonreligious person is as great as that of the religious person. Here the university has power and authority to make a singular contribution. Here the college chapel comes into its own, not primarily as a Christian philosophy club but as a congregation committed at once to the faith as true and to the clearest possible expression of this faith in a context in which a responsible denial of that faith cannot be treated either with cheerful indifference or passionate abuse.

VIII

The principal aim of the university is to assist actual persons to realize such of their positive potentialities as depend upon the refinement of their powers of reflection. The university, accordingly, is not licensed to create (or even to try to create) ideal persons — " a loftier race than e'er the world hath known." The university is not chartered to be an arbiter of taste in any respect or connection, though this does not prevent many of its people from so advertising themselves. In itself it is not a creator of values and it is not the judge of all men. Yet no human activity is foreign to its purposed inquiry. Unlike Aristotle, it is not " the master of all who know "; but it examines minutely what is claimed for knowledge in any connection.

Other aims seem now more clamorous and more fit to rule, such as vocational training and research. As subordinate, these aims are respectable. As imperial, they are intolerable. What a university has to offer vocational training is seasoned reflection on the ends of life rather than dexterities in its management and carefully tested methods for sifting testimony concerning the actual rather than blueprints for redesigning the cosmos. What a university has to offer pure research is a context in which human values are the supreme empirical reality that no experimental knowledge is permitted to threaten. Research that cannot accept these terms ought to find another home, or make its own in an otherwise uninhabited desert.

The university experience ought therefore to be an integral part of the humanizing process: that part which consists of the development of the reflective powers. As it turns out, the university has become the prime institution for the advancement of knowledge. Even its philosophy faculty is outraged or embarrassed, or both, to be charged with the awesome responsibility for fostering wisdom. So far as the university honors this function, it does so by dispersing it throughout the ranks to whoever will accept it, and thus confuses wisdom with presumption, charisma, or administrative skill.

God, or the unconscious wisdom of the university, has not given up. Since nothing in its life is more important than the confrontation of the ultimate options concerning man's being and his good, the grand debate goes on. It is as much in the interests of high religion as of the most secular of institutions to see to it that the grand debate takes place in the open. I believe that the avowedly Christian university has a distinctive contribution to make to this end.

Chapter Two

THE ARTS AND THE SCIENCES

I

We began with a distinction between unreserved and absolute commitment, and early found reason to believe that unreserved commitment does not necessarily diminish or obscure the most rigorous cultivation of reflective prowess. Just as early we have found it necessary to wonder where the burden of responsibility lies for the cultivation of the reflective powers. Now is the time to train that concern upon the traditional division of the university into the Humanities on one side and the Sciences on the other. It may be that the perpetuation of this division and the philosophy underlying it are sources of confusion.

But is it not prejudicial to speak of a *division* of the university when a widely prevalent form of faculty organization is there to deny the suggestion? Long live the Faculty of Arts and Sciences! — proof that *The Two Cultures* is mistaken. We may nonetheless legitimately ask whether Arts and Sciences is all *that* coherent as an educational system. In this case the question thinly hides a conviction, namely, that a serious division runs through the heart of the Faculty of Arts and Sciences. This sector of the university is an uneasy coalition of teaching forces formed to give the indispensable minimum of information and critical prowess to every undergraduate, except for the universities that now encourage students to study what they want rather than what their onetime mentors believed would be good for them. Moreover, the uneasiness of the coalition flows from an unresolved argument over the place of everything but science in the cognitive enterprise. In the realm of knowledge the place of science is assured past all common-sensical doubt or philosophic cavil. " To what shall we liken Science? And what can approach her honor and beauty? Brighter is she than all the stars of the firmament." Such raids on Biblical sentiments, in ancient days the tribute of piety to Wisdom, are seen warranted by the simplest facts of university life. That piety survives in the university as a specimen to be analyzed and explained rather than as a virtue to be emulated. In its place a great discomposure thrives, and grows from more to more. This malaise attends the question about inferences running from science to public policy. Where might one look now to find a science wholly immune to the bite of such a question? What is the science that can tell us how to track down the *right* policy inferences? Scientists have been wonderfully ingenious in instrumenting the policy decisions made by lesser men. If, for instance, we want as a people to see to it that everybody has enough to eat, scientists can and surely will tell us how to do that. We may need to look longer and harder to find a scientist to show us how to get the requisite legislation through the Congress. That too is a matter of instruments. And to what scientists should we turn when as a people we do not know how to choose among conflicting aims all of which are good. It would be very hard to believe that the nation ever needed great wisdom in high places more urgently for that ordering of priorities in commitment of resources, human and material, which will bring peace and justice in our time. But what arm of the university has revealed that wisdom as its attribute — or even as its aim?

Given the most widely pervasive understanding of knowledge and truth, the practitioners of the liberal arts still have important work to do. When the most momentous questions are raised, questions such as, " to be, or not to be " or in any case, how to be, either the specialists in the liberal arts speak their pieces or they should be dismissed for nonfeasance in public office. They are the fathers and sons of a grand conceit: Theirs are the humanistic studies, their ultimate subject is man himself. Humanistically understood, man is not something to be analyzed into his constituent elements, the same thereafter to be subsumed under laws covering, in principle, every element and event in nature. Man, rather, is a creating being and he is a being who makes judgments about the value of his creations. Not the least of his creations is a body of knowledge on which he, rather than Heaven, bestows the lovely accolade of Truth. (We do not pause here to puzzle over scientific theories of knowledge that in principle make even *this* a function of nature.)

Thereby the task of the humanist is made uncommonly difficult. Now he is under professional obligation to provide at least an outline of a system of value that incorporates whatever is true in scientific knowledge, and this system must be man-affirming in ways clearer and richer than the sentimental salutes to the importance of being human in which even the most incorrigible reductionist may indulge without serious self-contradiction if for nothing else than to help settle his Sunday dinner. But this does not mean that the humanist is called to sanctify the existing order. Nor is he obliged to bless everything that promises to disrupt the existing order. It is his business to consider in public how the human commonwealth can best be served. What he knows, wherever he learned it, ought to be imbued with prospicience, so far as his subject matter is really humanistic.

Prospicience is concern for the future of a human entity. It goes beyond both prediction and prophecy. As an attribute of humanistic understanding, prospicience relates as properly to the future of the existing value system itself as it does to changes within the system made possible by the system. But it is not humanistic business to guess what is going to happen next either in or to that system. The humanist ought to be proficient in tracing ways by which expectations created by the system can be met more adequately even though the system might thereby be altered. Beyond this the humanist ought to ponder how the ways hit upon for producing optimal satisfaction of these expectations can be generalized for the benefit of the great human world.

Undoubtedly this is hard and hazardous work. How much more simple and comfortable it would be if it were a matter of exporting American democracy to the farthest corners of the world! But having learned, and this at heavy cost to others as well as to ourselves, that people do not pass gracefully and gratefully from tribalism into democracy, American style (or any other, for that matter), we must not fall back into cynicism, despair, or self-pity. As a people we are prone to imbue our corporate presence in the troubles of other people with overwhelming salvific value. We are strong to save even though the beneficiaries are reluctant to yield and may in fact retort, " Physician, heal yourself "! Whereupon priests and prophets unite to lead us into an orgy of self-accusation. Apparently whatever we go in for we must lead the pack: if not in righteousness, then in wickedness.

There is a more excellent task. That is to delineate carefully and fairly the contradictory expectations that American society creates and blesses. Now these contradictions have been consolidated into severe crisis. Before crisis can be appropriately resolved it must be adequately understood. The humanists must expect that people will look hopefully to them for assistance in this. If the humanists have only passion to offer, albeit profound and noble, they will have failed. When we need a new vision we cannot be content with a confession of outrage.

Thus the sector of the university most vulnerable to the pressures for relevancy is the liberal arts. The sciences are largely responsible for this situation. Science begins as a desire simply to learn what is the case. Desire to master nature comes along soon enough, and in the modern world this desire is so obvious and so powerful that it can easily be read as the dominant appetitive essence of science. Nonetheless the desire to have truth so securely grounded that one can contemplate it as though it were eternal lives on. The popular mind may find this odd or even dangerous. It is neither. But Western civilization is becoming a massive conspiracy against this noetic aspiration. Somewhere along the line " the Western mind " became obsessed with the importance and the possibility of changing nature, man included. Thereafter science emerges as the providential technique for making changes, teaching us the shortest distance between the given and the desired, and thereby the guesswork can be taken out of revolution. The cost remains, but if the computer cannot manage it, why should we?

Some branches of science have not yet been seized by this obsessive desire to change the world. There the unreconstructed noetic appetite still rules, seeking answers to questions the everyday world has not asked and cannot comprehend. That is all right. No one in the everyday world expects to be blown out of this life by a technological application of scientific discoveries about the sex life of the dung fly. Yet it is foolhardy to be dogmatic about this because the everyday world may be profoundly affected by philosophical appropriations of science that defy technological conversion. Do you really want to know why we behave as we do? Then study the apes; or perhaps even the dung fly is instructive. Granted, this is loose philosophy. It does not explain why people study apes and apes do not study people. But that is academic philosophy. Since it does not sell very well, it can hardly be important.

How, then, does either kind of science heighten the relevancy anguish of the liberal arts? Well, if humanistic studies cannot teach one either how to change the world or how to penetrate its secrets, what value can they have? If the academic historian can tell us the *real* story about the English middle class in the early years of the nineteenth century, why should we put up with Jane Austen's *Emma*? Moreover, if the humanists cannot or will not tell us *what* to believe, why should we be interested in their recommendations of norms for the appraising of beliefs? Finally, if humanists are not personally engaged in translating their beliefs about man and their hopes for a truly humane world into action calculated to produce a better life for all (if not now, then in the foreseeable future), why should we be interested in their interpretations of any segment of the prevailing system? Lacking that engagement, their interpretations give off the sound and smell of rationalizations, and someone has taught us that rationalizations are self-justifications.

Thus the sense of crisis confronts every branch of learning avowedly humanistic. Science shows us how to change the world and man. Where are the authentic prophets and seers — the diviners of wisdom and righteousness — to fix the goals of change and flay us with whips of scorpions when we wander from the path of rectitude and go whoring after false gods? The questions are accusative spears sticking into the flanks of the humanists.

But with good reason? There's the question. I have argued that the humanists are primarily responsible for the development of the powers of criticism. By " primarily " I have meant that they are more responsible for this than anyone else in the university. This does not mean that humanistic scholars have nothing else to do. Whatever else they do or aspire to do as technical experts cannot be more important, and it ought not to be done at the expense of criticism.

What, then, ought we to say about the humanistic work of interpretation? Quite as much as criticism interpretation can claim to be the heart of the humanistic enterprise. That way of putting it assumes that the two things can be separated, and that is wrong. Interpretation can be distinguished from criticism, but the one ought not to be separated from the other. When we consider the content of interpretation in its most general terms the interdependence of interpretation and criticism ought to be apparent.

I suggest, therefore, that the content of interpretation is the significant and signifying past. " Significant " is synonymous with " important." What importance has it for us, but for us not simply as ostensive human subjects, that is, as denizens of the everyday world? " For us " designates moral agents and creative individuals. The past is important for us because unless we learn to read it rightly we shall not know who we are. If we do not know who we are, how shall we divine where we ought to be going?

Interpretation is also fixed upon the signifying past. The past belonged to others before it belongs to us. But when we talk this way we are talking about the contents of human life and not primarily about their temporal relationships. This is to say that what we receive and value as our past was once held by human agents in the mode of prospicience. Then as now (that is to say, essentially) human life is lived forward. Human life is aim. But it is also achievement, fulfillment, realization, consummation. Thus the grand paradox of historical existence confronts us. What is achieved by prospicience adequate to the time or occasion is transmitted forward. What is transmitted is itself past. This is certainly a strict necessity of transmission. I cannot hand on what has not happened and I have no motive for handing on triviality. I can recommend the attitude of openness to the future. That recommendation makes no sense unless it is backed

63

by evidence showing that openness to the future is an essential ingredient in important realizations. We have in fact no choice but to be open to the future so far as we can act at all. So the recommendation, Be open to the future! really means, Look out for novel ways of receiving and transmitting the past. But it might also mean, The future is in God's hands; therefore be ready to hear and to obey him.

The last suggestion is surely an odd one, no matter how frequently it occurs in Christian history. We must grapple with it but not before we attend further to the concept of the signifying past.

Humanistic studies ought to inspire the question, What was this past (this history) to the people who had it, made it, and were made by it? This is of course to ask, Who were they, anyhow? Idle curiosity can toy with that but cannot get anywhere with it, except fantastically. Disciplined inquiry may get somewhere with it. Part of the requisite discipline is a metaphysical belief (which can be dressed out as a scientific hypothesis) : The people signified by this past were members of the human commonwealth, together with us and all that is yet to be human.

That is why curiosity flits across the surface of their story. That is why disciplined interpretation probes for its heart. Moreover, the essential reason backing this metaphysical belief has very little to do with the exact science of paleontology. The past is humanly signifying only so far as it has left us intentional signs. These may be very abstract, e.g., uniform ways of burying the dead. They may be very concrete, e.g., literary monuments. In any case interpretation is activated in order to tell us what these things meant to their creators.

It is easy to remember or to imagine the vivid shock a claim such as this produced when it was first heard. " Impossible to do that! About that, one can only guess. About that, science is shrewd enough to be silent."

Perhaps the sole virtue of that reaction is to call attention to the close relationship of *significance* and *signifying* to each other. The humanist historian does not need to hypothesize extravagantly. He does need to have access to a working model. He does need to know what a personal agent, a value creator, is. He does not need to have a complex or abstruse theory about Symbol. Rather, he needs to know what symbolizing activity is. More specifically he must know how interpretation itself is a creative as well as a critical enterprise. That is, the historian must tell a story in which the fragments of that story first told long ago come again into unity. He cannot be altogether certain that the new unity is identical with the old, but the margin of uncertainty has little in principle to do with gaps in the evidence. The new unity is necessarily infused with novelty generated by *importance*. Thus the historian can legitimately aspire to authenticity, but he has no right even to dream of identity. He is obliged to be faithful to the evidence. Another faith reaches out for him, and that is what has here been identified as an unreserved commitment. Historical hypotheses can be modified by new evidence, or by another look at the old evidence, or by a more elegant argument. An unreserved commitment can be dropped. Thereby a person evacuates one history and moves into another: he plans to change his life and hopes to change the world. A vision of a better world may be the decisive cause of such a movement. No earthly power can guarantee that the subject of it will survive the ordeal.

II

The university is widely celebrated as the place where all faiths are tested and none is officially endorsed. It is the high calling of the university to scrutinize all gods and worship none. This is the great divide between the free and the bound university.

Ought we to infer from this that the free university does not endorse any unreserved commitments? Doubtfully. The very idea of the university embraces an unreserved commitment to the life of reason. Are we not threatened therefore with a lethal self-contradiction? The free translation of " test all things and hold fast to that which is good " emerges as " the university can carry you no farther than an unqualified endorsement of that self-awareness which is produced by self-criticism." Surely here we can see the makings of an escape from self-contradiction, for here the university stands forth as unreservedly committed to a posture and to a process but not to a content and specific result.

How happy the life of a university if facing up to such self-contradictions were its most severe anxiety! Clearing out a thicket of nonsense about the university's having faith in Reason may not advance the advent of that age, but it is an honest obligation nonetheless. We can reasonably hope to do this by (1) reducing the magnitude of Reason to reason, and (2) by insisting, again, that the proper object of an unreserved commitment is personal: first, actual persons; and thereafter, surrogate persons. From there we may be able to see that the gods subject to the unsparing criticism of the university are not ultimate objects of loyalty. Rather, they are policies and policy-supportive beliefs of a metaphysical order. From there we should be able to conclude that the proper business of the university is not to change the religion of its constituents. Something much more difficult remains to be done. That is to deepen awareness of the implications of one's faith, whatever it is.

As though this were not enough for which to accept responsibility, the people of the university appear to ask for more. Where but here can we be exposed to the heights and depths of the religious options spread before the human community — where but here in a conscientious and properly disinterested way? The student from Kansas may not find Islam to be a real option for him, especially if he is going back to Ottawa. Nonetheless it would be good for him to know that being a Muslim may be just as hard work and in this life, at least, quite as profitable as being a Southern Baptist, and that one would not need to be a lunatic first to be either.

1. The reduction of Reason to reason begins with attending to actual human beings struggling to be as reasonable as possible about whatever matters most. Metaphysical Rationalism may well survive this alienation of affections, but that is not the issue. Perhaps good reasons may be adduced for believing that ultimate reality is an absolute mind and an unbelievably logical mind at that. The reasoning faculty in man is not a very good reason for accepting such a belief, not because there is no such faculty — surely an absurd opinion unless " faculty " is intended to be a ghost smasher — but because human reasoning is a great variety of mental activities from which we can extract one such to serve as the norm for all only by begging the question. This is no obstacle to plausible and perhaps sound generalizations about reasoning. I am, for instance, reasoning when I am able and willing to follow abstract pointers in order to figure out something. One such pointer is implication. It is not reasonable, however, to forsake all other pointers and all other routes to cling only to this one. It is the dictate of reason to let in the pointers appropriate to the case. There must be rules of evidence, but the rules cannot produce the facts.

Accordingly Reason signifies an ideal relevant to the efforts of actual persons trying to be as reasonable as possible. " As reasonable as possible " is dictated as much by the manifold contexts in which reasoning is called for as it is by the uneven distribution of reasoning power in human beings or by the wide range of convictions about the value of the ideal Reason. How reasonable should a person in love be about his love and about his beloved? What are the dictates of Reason here? Perhaps, " Don't do anything from passion alone." But love is a passion. Moralists may talk it around into a policy, but first and last love is a passion. Well then,

how about this: " Don't love a person who shows he is unworthy of your love "? What constitutes enough evidence
that a person is not worthy of my love? Perhaps little Isaac
had all the evidence he needed when he saw father Abraham
raise the terrible sacrificing blade. Who has the word
straight from Reason that Abraham at that moment had lost
all claim to love, even if we were sure that love is a claiming
thing? Is Abraham's testimony irrelevant? Or Isaac's? Or all
Israel's?

Surely religion is another context in which some try to be
as reasonable as possible. One of the results is theism. So
what are the dictates of reason when a religious person is
trying to follow the commandments of God? To what court
is he accountable when he says that he has reasons for believing in and obeying God? Again Abraham: Is he acting
reasonably when he packs off for parts unknown, leaving
security, good name, and a going civilization behind, forever behind, so far as he knows? Or Jesus: Is he acting reasonably when he persists in moving the action right into the
lion's mouth, " setting his face to go up to Jerusalem "? Unless we want to fall back upon scientific (or perhaps even
metaphysical) theories about religious compulsions, we can
only concede, however reluctantly, that the kind or degree
of reasonableness proper to reign as a norm in or over a
human situation must be learned from the situation and not
finally from abstract descriptions of the situation, but from
the most painstaking inspection of the testimony of the
participants.

What ought one to be looking for in that inspection?
Surely what the participant believes he is doing. He says,
" I am obeying God." To this one may of course reply,
" How do you know you are doing what God demands? "
What would a reasonable answer from the participant be?
" God told me "? or, " God told somebody whom I wholly
trust "? Either answer seems to be more reasonable than " I
don't know what God requires of me but I *think* this is

what God would tell me if he did get in touch with me or with somebody wholly to be trusted." If we import into this situation an abstract scale of rationality, the last of these answers seems to come out best, but only because it indicates a readiness (and perhaps a skill too) to deduce a conclusion from premises that may or may not be true but the function of which can be clearly specified. Thereupon we would need to vindicate our decision to import the abstract scale of rationality. To do that we would be obliged to indicate the context in and for which that scale is binding upon all parties.

It is not too difficult to make a prediction about that context. It will be something called philosophy. More specifically, it will be philosophy in the university. The philosophic sector of the university is the context in which the fullest recognition of the claims of reason is to be expected. This does not mean that the best thinkers in the university are all members of the philosophy department, though chance distribution might bring up that combination. Rather, the most articulate and cogent expression of the demands of the ideals of Reason has generally been an explicit and overt philosophical aim.

Fortunately this fact does not entail making the philosophy faculty an object of unreserved commitment. Otherwise the professional ghost smashers and god chivers would themselves emerge as idols, either individually or corporately.

2. And yet the proper object of an unreserved commitment is personal: either a person or a surrogate person. In such a commitment one decides for the good of a person or persons, and the decision is meant to be binding. That does not make it religious. When such a commitment is accepted as God's will, indeed his positive commandment, one has entered the religious context. This is even clearer when one believes that God is engaged in something like this kind of "self-involvement," or when one construes reality as bend-

ing to comprehend and not merely to allow such affairs.

Policies are material inferences generated by unreserved commitment. There is no difficulty in conceiving a faith that does not set off policy inferences. That would be something other than unreserved commitment. Faith in this sense, faith so understood, without policy is a matter of verbal declarations. These declarations may suggest a disposition favorable to the good of others. But they may exhaust that disposition, leaving no fuel for more significant action.

On the other hand, really to be for the good of others calls for the projection of a concrete and elastic purpose into the future and over an indeterminate variety of actions. That is a policy. It is a pattern by which a promise, a decision-to-be-for, is and is to be enacted. Thus a policy is more than a tendency to act in such and such a way. Policy is settlement upon an appropriate tendency. It is a chosen habit rather than a reflex that happened and happened to be lucky and agreeable as well.

Policies are the gods that the university examines with the greatest possible rigor. But why use " gods " this way? Because policies tend in the minds of their proponents to harden into immutable, irreversible, and eternally adequate substances. And because the beliefs invoked, or perhaps even generated, to support policies often have a perceptible religious quality. " Liberty and justice for all! " is read out both as a law of nature and as the revealed will of God. Indeed policies far less benign are often given the same kind of backing. It would be hard to think of a policy designed for the public world that has not been so supported with the utmost sincerity. Sincerity displayed in a dubious cause is a great inducement to cynicism. That may well blind one to something both obvious and important, and that is the deep desire to believe that somewhere there is a policy certified as good by the courts of heaven.

How, then, are policies to be tested in the courts of the

university, the same being certifiably human?

a. Policies are submitted to the test of factuality. Is a given policy sufficiently responsive to the facts? The question is a hard one. The facts at stake are never all the facts there are. But the important facts are not all available either. A policy is something designed to cover future events and persons not yet visible — they are not yet born or their interests are not yet clearly defined in relation to our present powers. Sound policy, nonetheless, must be reasonably responsive to this odd situation. Trivial facts can be safely ignored in the formulation of policy, provided that we are sure they *are* trivial, but it is not always easy to pick out and discard the trivial ones. Makers of policy learn that some of their constituents have made heavy investments in trivial facts. It is important for the makers of policy to know whether or when those constituents will make trouble, and how much. That is one kind or range of fact which makers of policy cannot afford to ignore.

Critics of policy ought to ask whether a policy adequately covers or allows for the relevant facts. But critics may not have access to those, or perhaps their access is significantly different from that of the makers of that policy. Thus the critics sometimes can reasonably go no farther than a hypothetical judgment: If such and such is the case, then policy X is wrong.

b. Policies are also subject to moral judgment. Designed to produce good, a policy may produce more evil than good. Or it may produce a kind of evil more to be deplored than the good of its design is to be commended. Its defenders may claim that genuinely unforeseeable events intervened and derailed a policy sound in principle and appropriate to the situation at the time. On the other hand, critics may be able to show that the policy was defective in principle, and only genuinely unforeseeable events prevented greater mischief from flowing from it.

c. Prudential factors also play a role in the assessment of

71

policy. Is this the right time for policy X? This question is sometimes correctly translated as, Can enough of the right kind of support be marshaled for its adoption? But it might also mean, Can we afford it? Questions like these are frequently leveled at programs, but they apply to policies as well. A program is the last link connecting a moral decision to the actual world. Policy is the intermediate link. Policy therefore catches it from both ends. So one hears a criticism like this: " It is all very well to help the poor, but I wonder about the policy of helping the poor at the expense of the rich." This might mean: " I think it unlikely that you will be able to sell this policy to the rich, though it would be a good thing if you could." But it might mean: " I don't think it is fair." There the moral factor emerges from the ostensibly prudential one.

Criticism also reaches into the bag of beliefs adduced to support policies. Here the picture changes a bit. The free university does not endorse any one belief or any particular bundle of beliefs. The members of the university are free to believe what they will or must, and the university ought not to create unnatural embarrassments inhibiting freedom to say what they believe. Very well. But what kind of testing of supportive beliefs does the university license as one of its unique operations? Or is it best understood as a context of maximum freedom of inquiry into beliefs, maximum not on some absolute scale but simply as the best available in this society?

If the interpretive work of the university is being done well, the variety of connections linking belief with policy will become evident for anyone willing and able to follow the game. When the interpretive work is done well it will surely bring to light the fact that some kinds of belief have, and have necessarily, a mysterious connection with policy. So if a mysterious connection is advertised as a reason for adopting or supporting a policy, it would be reasonable to decline to accept that reason, even though we might accept the policy on other grounds. Suppose, for example, a person says he is in favor of " justice for all " because he believes that reality is a mental system. Now reality may be a mental system, and " justice for all " strikes many as being an excellent policy, but the connection between the two is mysterious. Our hypothetical person may be held firmly to the policy by his metaphysical belief. If we judge the policy to be a good one, we may be grateful for the mysterious connection. A consequent readiness to recommend mystery would be excessive gratitude.

The university as such does not aim at the reformation of policy or of conduct as the natural and unavoidable objective of criticism. It harbors people who are dedicated to the reformation of the social order. They ought to be free to elicit and organize support for such causes without fear of reprisal from the controlling powers of the university. The university is also native ground for people who are opposed to sweeping changes in the social order, though they are probably considerably outnumbered by the liberal forces. They have as much right to freedom from suppression as do the prophets and apostles of a new order. Idealism is not the monopoly of reformers.

III

There are different ways by which a university may be committed to theological argument. These can be divided into formal and informal. Universities with departments of religious studies, and those with seminaries, are very likely to be committed to formal theological argument. What are the merits of Tillich's theology? What is one to make of the theological advertisement of God's death? Why has so much of current theology been so heavily influenced by existentialism? Questions like these arise naturally where theology is pursued under its own colors both in the classroom and outside it.

Other kinds of theological discussion come to mind. One

can ask questions about theology, such as: What kind of language is theology? What kind of logic is displayed in theological discourse? How do theological convictions function in the direction and assessment of human life? Questions of this order can be pursued seriously and profitably even if staunch supporters of standard religious doctrines are nowhere to be found on the faculty. But can they be answered without showing one's own theology? If, for instance, a philosopher dismisses Christian supernaturalism as an unreasonable view, would it not be reasonable to suppose that he is one of several things himself: (1) a theological skeptic (no case for any kind of God can be made good) , or (2) a proponent of some other view, a subscriber to some other metaphysical outlook? Admittedly, pursuing the matter might not be unusually rewarding. Much would depend on the readiness of the philosophical critic to acknowledge what he is after and to declare the weapons with which he hopes to bag it. His theological interests may not run beyond showing that things are not always what they seem. He may not have any public curiosity about why things act up this way. If so, it would be impolite to badger him.

Informal theology holds sway where people are prone to decide theological questions by appeal to nontheological theories they believe to be true. As an illustration of this I suggest a very popular interpretation of the way religious beliefs function in value conflicts: Religious beliefs function as justifications for moral decisions rather than truth-claims filed upon reality. Thus, " God is love " is not really a belief about the nature of reality. It is a justification for my trying to love other people — surely an odd thing to feel that one must justify. Or it is a recommendation that one should love others. But where did the critic learn that this is the way theological beliefs work? Did he listen carefully and well when the religious man said, " I feel I ought to love others as God loves me and I know that God loves me"? Granted, it might be the case that this lover of mankind, this follower of Jesus Christ, feels under pressure to vindicate his policy, not against the accusation that it is illegal or immoral to love everybody, but against the accusation that he has set himself upon a course that neither humanity nor the great world beyond will honor. He might well reply to that accusation: "There you are most certainly wrong. Love is God's policy, and therefore it alone will ultimately succeed." Obviously this is a matter of belief, and of hope. But it is not more a matter of belief than its contradictory. As a hope it is surely different from its contradictory, the same being despair.

Such questions are developed with great sophistication by philosophers and philosophical theologians. Altogether they are a small fraction of the people of the university devoted at any given moment to discussing these matters. The larger company is much given to citing theories about man, religion, history, etc., as though they were facts. Freud or Marx or somebody has cleared up the mysteries. If we can find the courage to do so, we can now put away the last superstition of religions and go our way as free spirits. Let our beliefs run only to the limits of scientific knowledge, or if beyond that, only in poetic expression.

This attitude toward metaphysical beliefs often falls into an uneasy marriage with a pragmatic outlook. Religious skepticism seems so sane, so humanely tied to the needs and prospects of the here and now. But when heavy crises rattle all the windows in the value system, and the foundations begin to tremble, we look to see the Ideal glowing in the darkness. Now at last the cultured despisers see what religion is *really* about and what it is *really* good for! Buried beneath the detritus of myth and mystic lore there is a small but wonderful flame of ethical idealism. As ancient systems crumble, this divine light begins to glow in the horrid dust. It may not help to decipher a new moral code but it will inform and warrant our rejection of a corrupt social order. In that light we can see how shoddy a merely pragmatic policy or policy warrant is.

Thus the present moment in the university finds us with a variety of theological possibilities. It is not easy to know what to make of them.

IV

The university is the dominant model of a going cognitive enterprise. It may also be the control center of the cognitive empire in Western civilization. The university is therefore the veritable cockpit of value conflicts in the world at the moment. It remains to be seen whether the university is also the benign paradigm of rational humane and productive management of value conflicts.

But why, *therefore,* " the veritable cockpit "? Let the answer to that be put as a question. At what points do ethical policies impinge upon the cognitive commitment of the university, that is, the commitment to the advancement of knowledge?

This question haunts the scientific people. We may wonder what help they get from nonscientific people, for who can speak authoritatively to the issue of what are the ethical limits of scientific experimentation with human subjects? The call for authority is one with the call for wisdom, wisdom rather than power. It is not a question of who has the right to speak on the question but whose voice ought to prevail for the good of all, for freedom of speech does not create a correlative obligation in others to listen, heed, and obey.

Many believe they are qualified to speak with authority on such matters. But where is the consensus? We are agreed that no arbitrary or external authority (read: power) can solve these great questions — though an iron fist might settle them.

Confusion is much easier to find than the consensus. Here, for instance, is a specimen confusion. If the university could pool its variegated expertise in the cognitive realm, a suitable and binding solution to these great ethical questions would be forthcoming. To that end let us ask the experimental scientists just what they are doing to human beings and what they would like to do if the university could at last transcend the limits of conventional morality. And then let us ask what consequences should be expected from so modifying human life.

Would those consequences be *good?* Now who is the expert? To what authority should the symposium yield?

Here the lights seem to flicker. Whose good do we have in mind? Suppose that the scientific experts discover a foolproof way of making everybody happy whatever the human quality of the environment. Against what kind of fool is this device proof? Are these fools now around in sufficient number and power to jeopardize the success of the hedonistic scheme? Do we have the right to make what might prove to be an irreversible decision for posterity? Twentieth-century man has in fact made many decisions. They are the sorts of things that require justification and may never get it.

This is to say that contemporary civilization is well on the way in the scientific modification of human life. In this, second-degree experts are as fully implicated, if there is any comfort in that, as are first-degree experts. A city planner is a second-degree expert. He makes use of a variety of arts and sciences, not for the advancement of science but for the revision of a given environment. He is not consciously committed to the modification of a mysterious substance called Human Nature — no metaphysician, he. He is a social engineer. He is licensed to change actual human life. So he puts express highways where efficiency and economy demand, these being nonmoral norms. Thereafter when people whose communities have been destroyed by his asphalt decisions use dynamite to punctuate their criticisms, he can hardly be blamed, for now he stands in the wings as the tool of policy rather than as its creator and lord. Somewhat more plausibly and a good bit more honestly, he could admit that he is the victim of an exceedingly poor education. Somewhere along the line the university failed (home and church, too, perhaps), but the university had the last crack at him and muffed it.

This calamitous failure may not be evident in the grade record. See, in his sophomore year he got an honors grade in ethics, so we did something right after all. In fact he wrote a brilliant paper on a stock problem in the course: Given the plight of the Donner party, was cannibalism right?

Where then was the failure? His university never assumed corporate responsibility for putting him in direct touch with the immediate human environment as an essential element in his formal education. Of course he did some field study in sociology and in political science and in architecture. He also participated in the Good Works Program of the chapel. But he was not allowed (to say nothing of required) really to live in a troubled area of the city. He went there to have a scientifically hygienic look. After dark he went there to raise good collegiate hell, from the municipal consequences of which he was saved by an assistant dean and the campus police. But no one tried to help him relate his developing expertise and moral passion to the actual human lives in University City. Great pains were taken to make him a well-rounded person, a civilized creature indeed. So while he designs the New City, his hi-fi system (which this Da Vinci assembled himself, of course) supplies a sustaining background of Vivaldi, Purcell, or Ellington, whatever is in. And to his date he pleads the merits of Merleau-Ponty or Marcuse while she goes temporarily blind from pure boredom and wonders in burgeoning existential pathos whether an early and earnest bedding might not save both of them from a fate worse than death. Weep not for her, piteous though her plight. Weep rather for the faceless unnamed multitudes whose earthly fate he decides with transit, computer, and aerial photographs. And send not to ask who

78

taught him to practice this fatal dissociation of job to be done from life to be lived and thereafter to be justified or not. For the culprit is a corporation and its name is University, inexhaustible fount of knowledge and wayward mistress of wisdom.

The theme of Detachment vs. Engagement will require more serious attention than this. At the moment the question is less dramatic: Has the university properly acknowledged a basic fact of its own life, namely, that it is the cockpit of value conflicts in American life? Not that every such conflict can be found in the university. Rather, the university is singularly well-placed and well-endowed to state these conflicts in the clearest possible way and to throw maximum light on them. To do so is an obligation.

Rightly to discharge obligations of this order does carry the university into theological disputation. There are many indications that a great bashfulness, or is it weariness, has settled over the university. As a result theological argument is often disguised as something else. Does this mean that the explicitly Christian university has a real initial advantage in mounting theological discussion? That remains to be seen.

Chapter Three

INVOLVEMENT VS. DETACHMENT

I

It would be hard to imagine an issue more divisive than this one in the university scene. Indeed in the minds of many it is no longer an issue. Detachment has been tried and found guilty of gross negligence and has been sent into exile. Even those who have not accepted this sentence have often accepted the burden of proof for the preservation of the ideal of detachment. This is a moment when many traditional values are wilting before the fiery demands of justice at home and peace abroad. What right can the people of the university claim to remain above the battle and from that position pass judgment on its meaning and its cost?

If this is the situation in the secular university, should we not expect the avowedly Christian institution to be facing even more severe demands? For there one would expect an added impetus in the drive for engagement derived from the belief that the Christian is peculiarly bound to seek justice and peace.

That expectation is unrealistic. The Christian college may swathe the student in layers of protection against the harsh and/or seductive realities outside. Protection of this sort is not the same thing as detachment. But it has been argued that the purpose of the protection is to assure a climate suitable and propitious for serious reflection, a view congruent with the conviction that the purpose of a university is not "richness of experience" but the "examined life." Richness of experience is something the student must acquire on his own. The testing of experience, the criticism of life, is something for which he needs expert and sympathetic assistance.

Furthermore the adults in the Christian university may earnestly believe that such institutions have a stake in the preservation of this civilization. Indiscriminate attack upon the social fabric can, therefore, be persuasively represented as one of the greatest of all possible evils, since it may well spread to embrace God, church, motherhood, and virginity.

Yet even here the adherents of detachment have largely accepted the burden of proof. One of the standard ways of doing this is to show that the Christian — both the person and the group — is more responsive to the demands of engagement than anyone else. This may mean that the urge to act Christianly for the salvation of the world suppresses every need and every desire to learn how to interpret the world Christianly. Thus the seeds of anti-intellectualism already flourishing in the university are watered by the tears and sweat of prospective martyrs.

Any hope of profit from moving into this warm but frequently sterile controversy ought to be a modest one. And so it is. I hope to show that the Christian university has a unique and significant opportunity to reduce the heat and increase the light generated by the quarrel about engagement and detachment.

II

One of the less productive features of the controversy is the readiness of participants to caricature the opposing position. Thus detachment is represented as the last resort of indecisive, irresolute, and chickenhearted academics. The caricature has some plausibility. Is there a college anywhere

81

in the land that does not have at least a small handful of professors totally unfitted for life in the trenches or on the barricades? This could be accepted as a fact of life, and perhaps represented thereafter as a problem for Providence, were it not for the unremitting readiness of such unworldly incompetents to insist that they alone really know the score.

The friends of detachment are certainly not made up of such self-caricaturing creatures. Detachment may be the slogan (and disguise) of powerful and worldly men who have created or inherited an empire and mean to preserve it intact if not to extend its boundaries. For such detachment does not mean being removed from the world. It means being so dedicated to the needs and possibilities of one institution, or one kind of institution, that the condition of any other must be a secondary concern at best.

But to the opponents of the ideal, this too is represented as betrayal of a higher or more general good. How — so runs the charge — can intelligent and masterly people live in and for an institution that is parasitic upon the body of society, especially of urbanized society?

A still more persuasive objection is voiced as a plea for a more adequate educational method and theory. The traditional option made the most of " knowledge by description," and the descriptions were controlled, as far as possible, by the ideal observer: They were not to reflect partisanship or any other of the more depressing aspects of finitude. Thus few people can remember the author of a single text used in grammar school or high school. It is almost as though the subject, e.g., civics, had written its own texts.

Perhaps the traditional option was too much influenced by the ideals and the methods of science, early and late. Whatever the explanation, the situation is changing. Now the urban environment of the university is no longer viewed as a historical accident or as a laboratory for the social sciences. It is there as something to be learned about by systematic and ethically concerned participation in its life. Even the quasi-monastic living arrangements of the university are falling before new theories, new convictions, and new methods. The university is no longer a sacred precinct to which the student flees at the end of a bruising day in the world. It is the proper name of a constellation of human resources, of knowledge, craft, science, and art, for the rational resolution of human problems.

Thus the university has been swept into ever-greater involvement with clamorous life outside the walls. Characteristically learned and concerned people within are now producing philosophical justifications for this abandonment of the traditional option. When philosophers come around to this, the ultimate vindication of change, it would be reasonable to suppose that the battle has been won.

It would seem reasonable to suppose so. In fact, the battle still goes on, and any claim of victory would be premature.

Then to what caricatures of involvement do the adherents of detachment lend themselves? " Involvement! " is the cry of the passionately uninformed. It is the supreme justification of partisanship and of reckless defiance of responsible inquiry. It is an escape from that discipline which prepares one to consider all the options and choose the best of them. Involvement is the proper name for the hope that full-throated action in behalf of interests whose rightness is intuited will prove a negotiable substitute both for accurate knowledge of the situation and for careful testing of the various claims to rightness of policy for coping with it.

A more measured criticism of involvement is possible. For instance, it can be pointed out that the university has no peculiar or remarkable advantage as a launching pad for social reform. What the university can offer the surrounding society is an array of instruments for finding out what is so, and a company of trained critics. To the degree that the refinement of cognitive and critical resources is likely to change the face of the world, to that degree but no farther the university is part of a revolutionary process. There is nothing in the idea of the university, unless it be there by virtue of arbitrary stipulation, that requires it to assume a commanding vanguard position in the army of social protest. So the readiness of students to abandon study for the sake of social reformation is directly contrary to the purpose of the university. Somewhere along the line the best interests of the students have been betrayed, that is, as students. Something or someone has persuaded them that if the rightness of a cause is only felt deeply and simply enough in the gut, no argument against it or impartial analysis need be endured. Thus one of the unique values of life in the university is jettisoned, namely, a season of detachment for acquiring instruments of reflection and argument suited to an infinite variety of subjects and subject matter.

III

Recently we have been observing the playing out of this sterile controversy over the purpose of the university. Passionate avowal either of involvement or of detachment, at the direct expense of the other, is very like passionate avowal of the value of day or of night, but not of both. Beneath the controversy, moreover, one can detect a common assumption that the university offers preparation for something rather than the practice of something. This assumption is partly true and partly false.

It is partly true because the universty is engaged in training for professional service in society. It is partly true also because the larger part of the university community expects to leave it for life elsewhere. Thus for the students the university is a stage on life's way rather than a way of life.

The assumption is also partly false, first, because the climate of the university ought to encourage the practice and pursuit of its arts and sciences as values to be esteemed and realized without respect to the season of one's life. It is a sad commentary on the " real " world into which one is graduated from the university that it is often a severe step down from the high level of intellectual, moral, and aesthetic challenge of the academy. How happy we would be if this were merely a transition from monastic bookishness to the roar and heat of society's powerhouses! Or if it were the welcome though painful progression from playacting to the real thing. Unfortunately this is not predictably so. Too often one is graduated into intellectual sloppiness, and into the dire choice between aesthetic elitism or philistinism. Thereafter it is but a matter of time before one must expect one's own children to come in from college determined either to redo the house and the family from the ground up or to renounce the whole package forever. And one does not know which would be preferable.

The assumption is partly wrong for another reason. The university ought to be a powerful and resolute critic, indeed opponent, of that false eschatologizing of human life which reads the value of every moment and season out of (down from) some splendid consummatory end. It is, of course, true that the student is in process of becoming. But ought we to infer from that, or otherwise learn, that the professor has risen out of *becoming* into *being?* Hardly. What matters most in and for the university is the relative latency of creative and critical powers in the one and the relative mastery of such in the other. To that distinction the age difference is at best incidental, and so also are the other patented indexes of maturity. That is to say: The university does not aim at maturity as though it were the *summum bonum.* It aims at the perfection of expressive power, and acknowledges that this power can and must be used both to tear down and to build anew.

This means, incidentally, that very little work in the university ought to be assigned and treated merely as academic exercises — as trial runs — and, least of all, simply for the purposes of grading. There is no justification for asking students to think about something trivial for the sake of learning how to think. If, moreover, everything important and knowable is already known about, say, the Roman Empire, there is no use in encouraging the student to pretend that he is going to uncover something. On the other hand, if something problematical still lurks there, the student ought to be let in on it very early, for from this he may derive a sustaining and humane motive for mastering what is really known about it.

Rightly to identify and thereafter to oppose false eschatologizings of human life is theological business, whether or not it is so named. It is not the kind of theological business that can be done well and tellingly by bemused, overheated, and distracted minds if, indeed, any kind of theological business can be managed by such.

It does not follow from this that detachment ought to be elevated as a mode of life. It does follow, and it is true, that the well-ordered life, of Christian conception and dedication (or of either), must incorporate the disciplines of detachment.

IV

The Christian university should be able to make an important and perhaps a unique contribution to the discussion of involvement vs. detachment. This is not likely to happen if the university has been negligent in its fundamental theological work. The authentically Christian factor is something believed. It is a view from which appraisals of life in the world are drawn. Thus in an explicitly Christian context the pursuit of adequate understanding cannot be slighted in favor of a more passionate hand-to-hand engagement with the powers of darkness.

I suggest, therefore, that Christian involvement in the sufferings of present humanity begins with an acknowledgment of the human situation under God, and not with an irresistible stirring in the bowels of compassion. It has never been demonstrated that Christians *feel* the sufferings of mankind more keenly than non-Christians. What profit would there be in such a demonstration, for either Christian or non-Christian? Why should they not agree at the outset that man is endowed with a capacity for fellow feeling? And that this capacity is more richly developed in some than in others? And that social expectation and reward exert substantial influence in the generation and persistence of humane sentiments?

What then is the authentic Christian acknowledgment of the human situation? The core of it is the perception and affirmation of absolute solidarity. Man is one, and this by creation rather than by human self-positing or aspiration. Hence the ideal of harmony has a point of contact with the fact of the matter. Without this fact the Christian doctrine of original sin is nothing more serious than a bad case of rhetorical excess.

But where is the imitation of Christ to come in? Surely even in the university it is preposterous to hint that the practical piety of Christian people must be administered by professional theologians. This practical piety incorporates a marked anxiety over seeming to be remote from the struggles and conflicts raging in society. How could a Christian theologian presume to allay this anxiety? If he really honored Christ, he would scramble to the center of the action, he would lead the rush to the places where people are being most savagely hurt, he would intentionally inflame the anxiety and the guilt of the immobile uncommitted.

Might one ask here, What would he do when he got there? Perhaps just being there might have symbolic value; the real Christian puts his own life into the jaws that are grinding the flesh and bones of his brother man. Just as Jesus Christ offered his life for the blessing of mankind, so his faithful disciple offers his own life for the good of any, even the least presentable and ungracious.

Harsh occasions invite us to substitute passion for understanding or at the least to claim that the world cannot wait for us to acquire more understanding. So it is here. The practical problems of the hour demand our fullest engagement. Otherwise, what? They might destroy the world. Or Christianity will slide even farther down into irrelevancy and obstructionism.

Thus the dire alternative to Christian activism must be appraised, and not by emotion but by insight. More specifically the imitation of Christ has never meant one and only one course of action. Why should it now? A Christian who does not care for living persons is a sociological statistic. A Christian who says he cares but does not really care is a liar. But how do we learn that he does not *really* care? If we do really learn this, we do so not by plumbing his interior life but by inspecting and appraising the ways in which he disposes himself in the world, and by listening carefully to his interpretations of these self-dispositions. For while " the Christian thing " is certainly a registration of a clear preference for living one way rather than another, it is also a way of construing success and failure in the pursuit of the good life. Thus my confession of unrighteousness is as important a datum for judgment as my failure to vote the reform ticket. Judged in the light of world history, my confessed guilt for having defrauded a blind widow may seem trivial, but Christian moral judgment is not unreal for its having moved in such a narrow scope.

The fact of the matter is, nevertheless, that Christians in this democratic society are likely to have a cosmic sense of responsibility and guilt, or to feel guilty if they do not have such. A singular combination of immense corporate power with political democracy induces us to believe that the action of the individual is loaded with enormous consequences. If he is a good democrat, he is likely to feel that his vote, if not his counsel, may have world historical implications. So a normal aspiration — from which a normal anxiety and a normal guilt flow — to make some kind of positive difference to somebody is expanded to an immense magnitude — one might make a discernible difference to every-body.

Accordingly we have at least two items for theological scrutiny: (1) a radical revision of the image and estimate of the individual moral agent; (2) a radical revision of the eschatological horizons of moral action.

What has already been said about item 1 is not intended to conceal important empirical counterindications. One thinks of the common feeling that the voice of the commoner is drowned in the roar of massive institutions that steadily aggrandize themselves at his expense. Furthermore the world is run by and for bosses whose native endowments and good luck have lifted them far above his poor power to admire, envy, and hate across a chasm he can only dream of crossing.

The passion for Christian involvement is a fairly direct response to such sentiments, which can be found even in the university. " Now look: *You* are more important than that! God is no respecter of persons. *He* is not impressed by pomp and worldly power, so why are *you?* " That is one way of addressing the commoner. I doubt that it accomplishes much. It is too vulnerable to even a thinly tutored response: " That is all right for God, he doesn't have to work for them — perhaps he too has to live with their mistakes but he does not need to suffer them forever."

So Christian passion takes another tack. " The iniquitous giant can be overcome by a sufficiently ingenious and firm concert of pygmies. So if you really care about making a real difference, unite; and together we shall be able to hurt him enough to change his policies, leaving to God the amend-ment of his principles."

Now the sophisticated commoner often responds to this summons. But it breeds cynicism: The leaders of the passion-ate concert quickly come to resemble the Enemy and to pre-fer the company of the high and mighty to that of the masses and by sheerest chance begin to appear in stellar glory in the mass media.

Whatever their fate these addresses to the ordinary man are initially plausible because he has antecedently accepted a generalized image and constitutive estimate of himself. The world is a frightening and frustrating place because it alternately threatens and confirms these antecedent beliefs. Fundamental theological work is thus called for. And that is work which requires significant distance from passionate concern. This distance ought not to be construed as remoteness or isolation. It means, rather, a time and space for disciplined reflection.

In regard to item 2, the Christian community has been caught up in a radical eschatologizing of the horizons of moral action. Theologians and prophets are once again insisting that such is the supreme calling of church and Christian. The matter wants study and not at once a passionate choosing, confronting, and justification, of sides.

" Radical eschatologizing " means so staking out the end of human history that the vision and expectation of the End become the decisive criterion for the appraisal of human action. Thus all teleology bows before this triumphant purpose, and the guardians of the same have a certain divine right to decree the fate of all who oppose them for whatever reason.

There are powerful secular forces working for a radical eschatologizing of contemporary life. None is more powerful than the Marxist gospel. Part of its power springs from a singular combination of ethical idealism with brutal *Machtpolitik:* an idealistic reading of the End of history, and a readiness to use and thereafter endorse any instrument for the aggrandizement of the Party. That side of Marxism has a notable theological justification, namely, the ferocious indifference of history itself to personal achievement, private conscience, and tender sentiments.

The Christian and the Marxist share a potent enemy, an

90

outlook that to both must seem a heretical eschatology. That is an apocalyptic reading of the present moment. This is a formidable enemy because the great powers of the Western world could make this to have been the penultimate moment in human history. And the apocalyptic visionary needs only to be assured that we are living in the penultimate stage. Indeed, apocalypticism must have the penultimate as well as the ultimate. How could one acquire virtue and enviable position if the game were already over?

But now for the first time in history human beings can draw the fiery end down not by their sin but by their power. Old-line apocalypticism could only hope that God would no longer tolerate abomination. The new thing in the apocalyptical line does not need to deal with such imponderables. The mechanisms of destruction are stockpiled. All we need is the moment of careless anger or of blind cunning.

Christian and Marxist alike decry the garish seductiveness of the new apocalypticism. For both, the ultimate fulfillment of the human possibility is cosmologically assured, it does not depend upon the affections of men of good will. The human good may be defiled by human beings but the essential human community is invincible.

If an important element in the rationale for a Christian univeristy is the guaranteed opportunity to present the Christian outlook, then the call to Christian action is not weightier than the call to Christian reflection. For what is the point and the value of imitating Christ if one has not yet come to terms with the question of the reality of Christ? Here again social crises are represented as denying the right to disciplined reflection. " Surely we already know enough to act, and one of the things we know is that tomorrow may well be too late — either the world will have gone up in smoke or we shall be proved to have been eyeless and silent while evil raged at high noon." This is one of the modes of radical eschatology. But it is also a heady appeal to the desire to be in on the action. This desire leaps the generation gap with the greatest of ease.

We might note in passing that the rush to engagement, which so many now look upon as the essence of ethical and therefore Christian life, may itself be fairly represented as a recoil of the younger generation against the self-celebration of their elders. The parents of high school, college, and graduate students inherited from their parents the following tradition. " *I* was doing a man's work for a man's wage at the age of fourteen. So *I* had roller skates, bicycle, car, etc., only when *I* had earned them. But *you* have yet to earn your first honest dollar in any way except as a fellowship for scholarly achievement." Thus the parent represents himself as one who early and profitably entered the real world, and who now spreads his bounty gratuitously upon the undeserving.

Is it, then, so terribly strange that the beneficiaries show growing disinclination to accept any more of the package than strict necessity or callous opportunism dictates? *Their* way into the " real world " has got to be different not only because the world is different but because Big Daddy has insisted that *they* are different, different apparently past all understanding. Moreover, they believe they know how generations of Big Daddies have brought the world to the precipice of extinction.

Big Daddy, nonetheless, has put one lesson in all the way to the hilt: You count only if you *do* something. So start doing early.

Surely this whole phenomenon of communication, both all too successful and pitifully inadequate, demands the most sober and responsible analysis. I have no doubt that it is fitting to treat it as a scientific problem. But it needs also to be handled in other modes of objectivity and for other ends. Again, why should we doubt that scientific theory might illuminate this situation? There is no better reason to doubt that the indispensable clues for the correction of this situation will come from a mode of being together in which the power of understanding and existential concern so interpenetrate that neither surrenders to the other and neither threatens the other.

If the Christian university cannot or will not represent and commend that mode of being together as the " joy of all desiring," it is condemned to being Christian in some trivial sense. For that common life is not available either as an object of proper study or as a realizable ethical goal in isolation of either from the other.

V

Involvement vs. detachment has proved to be a confusing way of discussing the moral and intellectual climate of the university. This climate has been largely taken for granted until the very recent past. Apart from some regional and parochial differences, there has been a remarkably inclusive consensus on the atmosphere most conducive to the advancement of knowledge and to moral maturity. One need only call up for review a random sample of the great slogans to recapture an honest sense of that dominant mentality in and about the university, whether it was avowedly Christian or self-consciously secular. " A community of scholars," " Disinterested love of truth," " Preparation for a useful life," " The legacy of the Judeo-Christian tradition," etc. The language once conveyed the sense of a stable and coherent subculture dedicated above all to the pursuit of ideal aims but responsive in varying degree of enthusiasm to the relativities of a democratic pluralistic society.

This was only yesterday. When the revolt broke out, few realized how inclusive were its ideal aims or how indifferent, if not overtly hostile, were its leaders to the moral casuistry of the university tradition. Among much else brought under fierce attack the climate of the university stands out as a favorite target. This attack was of course directed against the long-standing habit of professing one thing and doing something irreconcilable with that profession. But the exposure of hypocrisy rampant in the ruling generation is at best a secondary objective. For if a person's principles are wrong, his hypocritical violation of them is an advantage to others, and one ought not to belabor him with hypocrisy to the point where he feels publicly shamed into following his own evil principles. So the revolting generation is spending its best ammunition upon the received principles encased in the traditional climate of the university.

Take, for instance, " disinterested love of truth." Is it not the case that the generations which accepted the sovereignty of this ideal assumed that the massive society beyond the gates of the university was a singularly happy, stable, productive, and just synthesis of diverse peoples? So it seemed. Now it seems that that grand assumption is in full retreat. This social order is not happy. It is not strikingly stable either. As for justice, the very word is an offense to people long and cruelly victimized, because it has been used to dignify halfhearted, insensitive, and unintelligent schemes for keeping the ship afloat, even though a frightfully large number of its passengers are below decks without light or air and with bilge water as the staple item on the menu.

Thus if disinterested love of truth is to survive as an integral part of the climate of the university, it will have to be radically transformed. For the truth to be so loved guarantees neither happiness to its pursuer nor permanence to society. Truth is no longer conformance to a fixed reality. It is rather responsiveness to the demands of the good. Accordingly the moral condition of the petitioner and postulant of truth again acquires profound significance. Indeed the rising generation is disposed to find salvific richness in truth, or to reject as true whatever is in principle nonsalvific.

Given this situation, the Christian university has an exceptional opportunity again to mount the Christian view of the interpenetration of truth and goodness. For while Christianity certainly has a lively concern for salvation, it imposes no obligation to look for salvation behind every bush and under every stone. Bushes and stones might be interesting in themselves. The faithful Christian aspires to praise God in all things but not on the assumption that all things tell the same story. We can indeed now praise God for the gift of an age and of a mind for which the theologian cannot provide the antecedent answer to every question, even if he would.

Among Christian institutions the university is best suited and endowed to free the pursuit and celebration of truth from the heavenly burden of salvation, of which the popular fascination with the " practical " and the " existential " are faint yet real relatives.

Finally I should like to suggest that the authentically Christian approach to the issue of involvement vs. detachment is to develop " participation " as the vital clue to action in the political arena and to investigation both of nature and of history. Participation does not determine what one is to do in the case of ethical action, nor what one is to find in the actual world, present and past. What it does is to leave the core being of the other, whatever the other is, intact. At the same time participation is a standing invitation to the other, again, whatever it is, to enter into a complex of relationships from which an increase of being may ensue. May, not must. Thus participation is nonimperialistic and nonexploitive. The other is not invited to become a slave or a satellite or an instrument or a colony.

Adequate comprehension of what is there as other cannot be achieved by intuition alone. Reliance upon one's intuitions or upon any other kind of immediate reading, is far better suited to the furtherance of one's own self-referencing interests than it is to the real interests of the other. This is why participation calls for the most rigorous development of the powers of perception, understanding, and expression. This development, in turn, requires freedom from the immediacies. And this is the essential meaning of detachment.

Theology and the Church in the University

Were we created to act on the strength of feeling alone or of passion alone, neither the benefits nor the hazards of detachment could occur to us. But we are not so constituted. Whoever thinks we ought to have been or that we ought to act as though we had been must make out a case for his convictions or be content to take his chances with *our* intuitions.

Later on we shall confront the question of the church in the university. Here we have come rather nearer the question of the university in the church, for that is the way such notions as participation and the " interpenetration of the power of understanding and existential concern " must seem to be tending. But I do not have in mind any subsumption of the university relative to the church, if by " church " we mean a visible denominational structure. In fact, the denominational creation of universities may be fairly cited as a piece of unconscious wisdom. Designed to promulgate and sustain Christian belief and Christian morals and to prepare people for professional service in the church, the Christian universities have long since become links on the transmission belt carrying " Judeo-Christian culture " from generation to generation. Which is to say that the Christianity represented has become increasingly broad, no matter how narrow the picture of it may have been at the outset. This may be called wisdom if the part of wisdom is dignified adjustment to environmental demands and opportunities. For the spiritual needs of the general society seem also to require less and less nourishment from highly differentiated religious traditions. So " church " has nearly become the name of any local shops where generalized Christianity is available, under different brand names, but the same basic product.

Thus it has come about that some of the historic functions of the church have passed out of the control, and frequently out of the practice, of the parish and into the Christian university or even into the university no longer or not ever Christian. One of these migrating functions is theology. Even the catechetical churches do little sober theological work in the parish. Others boast theological study groups, some of which are remarkably lively. But these good souls are discussing theology perpetrated by luminaries of various magnitudes, and as often as not in the interest of intellectual sophistication. So in the course of time the brightest and most persevering of these parish students may be able to discern the Tillich strand in the pastor's sermons, or judge how little he really differs with Barth, etc.

The most obvious place for the amendment of this situation is also the most promising: the university. For the aim of the university is real wisdom rather than sophistication. There, perforce, theology is not a high-level pastime but a serious grappling with options, each of which has singular difficulties and for none of which can any appeal to authority be decisive; the university rather than the detached seminary, because the important theological options are personally and corporeally realized in the university. They need not be invented or simulated. They are there to challenge and to be challenged.

In the next chapter we shall see that theological options are not always staked out and labeled as such. Here too the university situation is of one piece with the intellectual environment.

Chapter Four

THE UNIVERSITY
AS A THEOLOGICAL ARENA

I

Everyone knows that the formal academic study of religion has been expanding throughout higher education. State universities, hitherto supposed legally immune to such infection, are capitulating to it from coast to coast. Privately supported institutions are augmenting their resources in the field as rapidly as possible and are making great efforts to make the department of religion as academically sound as any other department. Even where new departments are not being created or existing ones expanded, interdepartmental programs are burgeoning and are being defended as adequate to the demands of the intellectual climate and to the highest criteria of academic excellence.

I do not believe that this academic development can be fairly interpreted as a vivid or powerful theological renascence. It is not to be deprecated on that account. Why should we not sincerely applaud and where possible abet even a belated effort to apply the most exacting and (one would hope) the most appropriate attention to the phenomena of religion? Religion is an inalienable element of the human story. Even if it should be a diminishing element in the experience and aspiration of Western man, *that* story itself merits the best sort of telling. Surely the death of the gods is as moving a spectacle as their rise from implausible beginnings.

Let us say again that all of this does not yet add up to a rebirth of theology in its own right. The principal reason for saying this is to be found in the focus of this academic development of religious studies. The focus is scientific, broadly understood. Knowledge *about* religion is the commanding objective. Religion is discussed and explained without evangelical purpose. The intent is not to make students religious, it is not to press for commitment or faith. Rather, the aim of religious studies is for the student to be well informed and properly critical. This amplifying of self-understanding and of responsiveness to the lives of other persons and other cultures is the dual objective of the academic study of religion. Here again we may well detect a grand assumption: When people are well informed and properly critical, they will be either religious or nonreligious in a richer and more humane way than they would have been without the liberalizing university experience. This assumption is a particular application of the basic conviction underlying the liberal arts. Just as it is not the business of the department of art history to make students artists or the business of the department of philosophy to make them virtuous, so also it is not the business of the department of religious studies to make students either religious or nonreligious. The overarching concern of the liberal arts is the mounting of the human ideal, an image and conception of the full human life. Every historically powerful religious community has construed the ideal in a distinctive way. Surely the scientific study of religion is not predicated on the assumption that these unique envisagements of man can be thrown into one pot and boiled down to a common essence. But are we not just as convinced that as students of religion we are not obliged and indeed we cannot afford to accept as normative the say-so of any religious tradition?

II

What, then, is the university after in seeking to help people think more adequately about religion? Let us try to pick our way through the likely answers to this question.

1. Prevailing secularistic ideologies are almost certain to desensitize people to the phenomena of religion. Thereby something importantly human is obscured. This is the fact that man's story is beset with mystery. No monkeyshines in biology laboratories or in concentration camps can dispel this mystery. Religion arises in this sense of mystery. Religion is the historic way of coping with it. So even where reductionist theory, scientific or philosophical, dispels the uniqueness of religion, there remains the religious outreach of human life to the mysterious world beyond, above, and beneath.

2. There is good religion and there is bad religion. The distinction is drawn in the hope that people will cleave to the one and abhor the other. But the distinction is concretely difficult to draw. Hence the importance of training people to think about their religion, or about their religiousness, in case they have been delivered from servitude to mere history.

3. It is a good thing (and perhaps even a salvific one) for people to see the deficiencies and errors in their religious commitments. This seems to be a particular application of the general maxim, to be liberally educated is to be humanely aware of one's own imperfections. Ideally, such awareness seasons one's appraisal of the shortcomings of one's brethren.

4. Much the same point can be stated more affirmatively. To think more adequately about religion may assist one to realize more of the potentialities of one's own faith. Surely, e.g., one profits from thinking about the commandment, " Love one another "; and from thinking about the meaning of human life in terms of love as its proper end.

100

5. To think more adequately about religion may enable one to temper religious zeal with rational restraints of various sorts, such as respect for the rights of others and for the health of the body politic.

III

A common thread runs through at least four of these answers to the question, To what end is thinking about religion dedicated? This thread is the desire to make religion socially responsible. "Responsibility" being a variable in any equation devised for concrete situations, we must rephrase it thus: The present social order is the indispensable criterion by which religious commitments of every hue and degree are to be appraised except, paradoxically, an unreserved commitment to the preservation of the present social order. This surely is one of the more sober and significant meanings of the catch-all term, "secularization." It would be premature to begin talking at once of the false gods created by the secular order, or to start looking to the East for the dawn of a new and brighter day breaking upon the night in which the human spirit has been persecuted by supernaturalistic myths. We are not yet willing, that is, to say whether secularization is a good or a bad thing. We are prepared to say that it is a ubiquitous and largely uncriticized phenomenon.

I have no doubt that "present social order" will offend those whose humanism is sustained by belief in an ideal order, by appeal to which the shortcomings of the present state of affairs can be ascertained and, perchance, ameliorated. If the pragmatic spirit of American life is (or is to be) rescued from gross policies of expediency and quick cash-in value, it is only because of an idealistic streak deeper and loftier than the pragmatic. Even granted the idealism, the arbiter of conflicting value claims, the critic of any or all human creativity, stands fully within the "present social order" when he sets himself to think more adequately about religion, his own or any other. This he does and must do unless he believes, and somehow demonstrates, that the present order of things (perhaps cosmic as well as human and terrestrial) itself stands under the judgment of the living God. Of necessity " somehow demonstrates " because the question about the human good is clearly not to be settled by any merely mortal say-so, whether or not this say-so is advertised as the fiat of the wisest of all creatures. It is just the wisdom that requires to be demonstrated. It does not follow that any kind of appeal to a culture-transcending good and power of being delivers the critic from the all-conquering embrace of the secular order. A more cautious acknowledgment is in order, however. The here and now which is the indispensable platform under the critic is not (and I should say *can not* be) the criterion by which the " good and evil " of the present order, the " here and now " is assayed. Necessarily we start from " what the modern man thinks," unless we are irredeemable antiquarians or dedicated obscurantists. But we are not bound to end there, or even to do our principal business with it.

The prime objective in the academic study of religion can therefore be reformulated. This objective is a confrontation with explicit theological positions understood as so many positions in the perennial debate over man's being and good. Such a confrontation is nearer the center both of the ideal of the university and of actual religion than are the prevailing objectives of science or philosophy.

As matters now stand, the debate over man's being and his proper good is muffled by many elements of university life and is trivialized by many elements of religious life.

One of the most potent of the muffling factors in both is the belief that there can be no real and rational disagreements about life-attitudes, ultimate beliefs, absolute presuppositions, commitments, etc. This notion itself is supported, and it may have been produced, by a remarkable confluence of two intellectual streams, " Freudianism " and

102

" Positivism." I have put quotation marks around these terms simply to indicate that they are being used here as labels. But I so use them because (and only because) they are themselves efficacious in the university and the church as basic convictions (or life-attitudes, if you will) rather than as clearly formulated theories and hard-nosed arguments. They are persuasive as atmospheric pressures; they are in the air breathed by all in the university. Where this air is felt to be salubrious, people are content to express their deepest convictions with a sublime assurance that they cannot be proved wrong, because rightness of belief has been reduced to sincerity or " authenticity." Thus freedom is defended as the supreme value of the university, rather than as a necessary condition for the discovery of truth and the realization of the good.

We ought to resist the cynical inference that people never defend so violently their right to be themselves as when they are the most uncertain and anxious about who they really are. For even in this cloudy way the theological issue is joined, the issue concerning man, his being and his good. Freud, for example, was not happy about civilization. He did not see a way out that was likely to attract the masses. But did he see a way that could be made rationally convincing even for the most refined and unfettered intellect? Ah, yes, he lifted high the banner of scientific reason. With it he gestured in the direction in which the world ought to move. But what does science know of *ought,* except to explain why we feel it?

The Positivistic component may no longer be clearly distinguishable from the Freudian, except by philosophers. Nonetheless it is a distinctive contribution to the muffling of the theological debate. Positivism certainly does not attack the very possibility of any rational arbitrament of conflicting truth-claims. It does persist in dismissing metaphysics, religion, morals, and art from any such arbitration. How then could we reasonably avoid the conclusion: The

103

more a given human interest matters, the less rational any debate (except about causal explanation) over it?

Again, our present concern is not with the relatively clear formulations of philosophers. We are considering the crystallizing of theories into doctrines and the diffusion of these doctrines into the general climate of the university and thereafter into society at large.

Thus it is a mistake to suppose that the scientific orientation of academic religious studies is an unequivocal triumph of intellectual freedom over parochial religious passions. Scientific accounts of the rise and proliferation of religious communities are significant contributions of knowledge. Philosophical accounts of religious truth-claims vis-à-vis (or versus) the truth-claims of science and of metaphysics, may indeed enrich the critical appreciation of religion or at least warn the student of intellectual snares and delusions. But what can be doubted, and what in fact I deny, is that the central issues in religion have been fairly dealt with or even addressed in these ways.

The overtly religious population of the university has not done very much to lift the central issues out of obscurity and confusion. In that sector it is all but axiomatic that to be religious is to be religious in a particular way. Thus scientists, philosophers, and even theologians, cheerfully discourse about religion as such, and about man as the religious animal, etc. But no one practices religion as such. No one is religious in any general sort of way. Many are vaguely religious, but that is not the same thing. So the religious animal is actually the Catholic, Buddhist, Methodist, or Jewish animal; most of whom would feel that "animal" does not help them very much.

I do not see how or why we should question the plausibility of this reaction. Our questions concern the finality of this reaction and the wisdom of the way it is expressed within the university. Within the university it obtrudes as a bias working powerfully against real theological debate. What would the committed man have to gain from such debate? Why would the unregenerate be changed by it? One can, of course, seek appropriate circumstances in which to confess one's faith, or to parade one's freedom from religious superstition. Neither is what we mean by a serious theological confrontation. Each is likely to seek fellowship in the appropriate mutual admiration society.

Unfortunately, theologians have not been rushing headlong into this breach, even in universities equipped with theologians sitting in endowed chairs and thus institutionally licensed to commit theology. One thinks of the dominant theological movements which insist so heartily upon the supremacy of Revelation (in the case, obviously, of Christianity) that no merely human levers or clinchers are admissible. To offer a " case for Christianity " in that theological atmosphere is to be guilty of bad faith, even if it were a good case.

Thus it must surely seem to many that God, as well as doctrinaire Freudians and Positivists, is very suspicious of reasons for believing in him. Perhaps we ought to be rather more humble than this. If no one has ever been changed (to say nothing of converted!) by debate, presumably only God, rather than Kierkegaard or Barth, *knows* this to be true. Perhaps only God *knows* whether any universal negative empirical proposition is true, but *that* supposition may be a superfluity, a horrendous overreach, of philosophic modesty.

So what ought to be the grand and supremely formidable theological debate goes on erratically. That it goes on at all says more about Providence than about academic wisdom. Not that people are not speaking their minds. There is no lack of that. But the audience is already committed, or it is merely curious. The university audience does not expect very much by way of direct address to the absolutely fundamental concerns of human existence, and it is not getting much. Mostly what it gets are weighty pronouncements on contingent affairs and increasingly acrimonious debates on public policy. These pronouncements are now made and defended with splendid accompaniment of self-righteousness. It is not enough for the culprits in the seat of power to be wrong. They must be entirely wrong, that is wrongheaded and wronghearted. They not only make mistakes. Their mistakes are the worst on record. They are not only arrogant. They are more arrogant than Caesar, Napoleon, Tiglath-pileser, Nebuchadnezzar, and Genghis Khan rolled into one. This is quite an achievement for a country boy from hardscrabble Texas. Who knows what he might have done had he got an earlier start, or had gone to Harvard?

But where in the contingencies are we up against necessity? What finally makes a policy good or bad? Shall we continue blandly to assume that everybody knows the answers to such questions? " What everybody knows " commonly turns out not to be true at all, and even when there is something in it a proper reformulation cannot be decided by appeal either to majority opinion or to the whimsies of a self-appointed elite.

IV

The university that has an explicit institutional connection with Christianity has an excellent opportunity to renew explicit theological debate. This is the case even where that connection has become fairly tenuous, perhaps now a matter of charter rather than of conviction. I do not expect that this suggestion will produce a tidal wave of enthusiasm in such quarters. There, as much as elsewhere, the intellectual style is often enough overtly antitheological. But intellectual styles ought not to be regarded as impervious to criticism and modification.

There are three obvious resources the Christian university has upon which to draw for a serious and explicit theological confrontation. First, the formal curriculum, both undergraduate and graduate (if any). Second, the official or institutional chapel. Third, the interconfessional " dialogue " on the campus. I shall discuss these briefly in the order given.

The restriction of the formal curriculum to the scientific and philosophical study of religion is arbitrary and unnatural in any institution that calls itself Christian in any sober sense. But as soon as explicit theological teaching is proposed, a question is fired in from the church as well as from the Committee on Course of Study: *Which* theology? Mention theology and liberals begin to hear the thunder of authoritarian guns, and conservatives begin to murmur that only the True Church is licensed to dispense sound theology. The temptation to start a fight between these companies is great but wicked. Instead we must remind both companies that there are various ways of doing theology, and there are several kinds of theology. Precise distinctions among the kinds are not important for the work in hand, which is to plead for a systematic delineation of the Christian faith, together with the display of the grounds upon which rests assent to the faith. I do not believe that theology in this mode is an illicit arrogation of churchly powers to the university nor the seed of some kind of academic or intellectual tyranny. Quite to the contrary, careful theological work of this sort requires the maximum of open-mindedness in every quarter.

Secondly, the official or institutional chapel is a resource for the theological confrontation. This does not mean that the chapel is to be thought of primarily as a debating society — there is little likelihood of its becoming that. It is more likely to go on being a showcase for displaying the best sermons of a band of traveling preachers and the platform from which the chaplain launches his latest social-action program. Neither of these uses of the chapel can be called theological except in a loose sense. The itinerant preachers may espouse theological positions but they are not available for sustained and serious theological argument. The chap-

Theology and the Church in the University

lains committed above all else to social activism may presuppose a theological (or an antitheological) position, but they are often far readier for political controversy than for theological confrontation. Perhaps they assume a theological-ethical consensus broader than the avowedly Christian community, and from this draw off moral imperatives and permissions. Or perhaps they assume an ethical nucleus in the secular order before which explicit theological prepossessions and arcane piety must yield.

In either case, or in both, there is something seriously amiss in the university chapel. Since the last part of this essay is devoted to the chapel, I can offer no good excuse for pursuing its deficiencies and potentialities at this point. Let us rather consider the third resource of the Christian university.

The very fact that it is still Christian offers a unique possibility to a university for theological discussion. An intensely parochial atmosphere will surely obscure, if not obliterate, this possibility, and this, paradoxically, in the name of religious seriousness. The proper cure for this unhealthy condition is surely not theological indifference or nonchalance. Why need we be content merely to admit rather than to capitalize real theological disagreements? They can be properly exploited only when these disagreements become overt, when, that is, they are recognized and pursued as theological.

This is not to say that all the big questions are theological, unless " theological " is extended to cover all metaphysical and ethical issues, a kind of generosity not to be encouraged. But theological issues are big questions. Persistent preference for traditional conceptualizations may effectively conceal the magnitude of the subjects treated. Insistence that the real meaning of the language is accessible only to the true believers may also diminish the prospects of serious and illuminating argument. These are tactical matters, and one must hope that they will not incapacitate theologians for speaking theologically to theological concerns and leaping gladly into argument on the big questions. It is a rare campus that does not have diversity of conviction and commitment sufficient for this purpose. Where it is lacking it ought to be imported. I do not mean that university administrations ought to be sure that Catholics and Jews are appointed to a Protestant faculty in order to represent their respective religious communities. I mean that there are theological questions behind the doctrinal and ritualistic peculiarities of the major religious communities. These questions in fact create divisions within religious communities and alliances beyond them.

An age enchanted by ecumenism is beginning to learn this. Religious controversy is breaking out within the boundaries of the historic communities as these communities become increasingly aware of the unity of the human kingdom — its unity in mortal peril and in the hope of glory.

The Christian university is a providentially available arena for confrontation on those theological issues which impinge most directly and forcibly upon the kingdom of man. Such a confrontation is incomparably more urgent than dramatically staged encounters of Catholics and Protestants, with a Jew in there somewhere to express the profound gratitude of all Israel for having been exculpated, somewhat belatedly, from the fearful responsibility for having killed God in or around A.D. 30 on the Christian calendar. Apparently Israel had to wait for this vindication until a clutch of Dionysiac Protestant thinkers could prove that God had actually died more recently.

V

What a church is and what keeps it alive and what to do with a dead one are theological questions I am not proposing to treat in this essay. Our concern here is the Christian university. In the university, Christian or otherwise, we should hope that the *religious* character of a religious community would be properly understood, whatever one did about it personally or existentially. Rightly to understand that religious character is to see that in a very important way theological arguments are " real " only in the context of an overtly religious life. But so far this is only to agree that one must really care how inquiry comes out. It does not mean, so far at least, that one already knows " how inquiry comes out." What appears to be the logical result of a process of inquiry may not be embraced, it may indeed be vehemently rejected. This does not mean that Piety and Logic made a bad marriage. It may mean that the inquiry marched off in good order from the wrong premise. Logic alone cannot make convictions cogent to the unconvinced. One may of course believe that with God all things are possible. But suppose that one does not believe in God? Or that one believes the wrong things about God?

Obviously the venerable issue of Faith and Reason cannot be disposed of in so summary a fashion nor am I proposing to do so. The point is theologically modest: The fundamental arguments (or evidences) of any religious community have a real and constant reference to God as he really is and to man as he ought to be. This dual reference is not itself the monopoly of any religious community. Let him who must, say, " Outside the church there is no salvation." But let that same man not be so foolish as to add: " Outside the church, no God and no man "; unless his church is already incorporated in God and man together.

There are, then, theological contentions that are properly aired in the unique arena of the university. In this arena authentic religious commitment can and ought to encounter sustained and serious criticism. This encounter is not most appropriately represented as the conflict of Faith with Unfaith, nor as the conflict of Faith with Reason. Let us put it in these terms, rather: Unreserved commitment can be properly counted upon to give rise to assertions about God and man. These assertions are discussible. If they are not discussible, they are not really theological at all. They may be profoundly affecting and nearer the heart of the matter after all. But that is a different question.

To discuss the discussible and to do it fairly: this is an intellectual responsibility of the faithful endowed with the capabilities proper to the purpose. There are such people in the university. They may be tempted to construe this responsibility as a demand to make Christianity intellectually respectable. Behold! even a very bright and learned person might subscribe to the gospel! If not in its traditional form, then in another one. Thus begins the quest for a version of the gospel, or a fragment of it, that is compatible with the knowledge and wisdom of the age. That is what an intellectually respectable faith often enough comes down to. If the generation gap were not so wide and dark, this theological give-away program would leave the student at the mercy of his professors. He would be obliged to look to his learned and sophisticated mentors to flash the signal as to what one is now permitted to profess in order to remain in the good graces of the right people, and to remain in obedient if not reverential contact with the spirit of the age.

The present turbulence on the college scene casts some doubt over the future of such dependency, at least in the area of faith and morals. I am not entirely sure that maturity, insight, and patience are predictable products of social upheaval of this sort, anywhere in the spectrum of generations. But it may have thrust upon the university the necessity of reviewing critically what it has been doing to make Christianity a respectable creed without encouraging its people to lock horns in doctrinal controversy. I think that the time for muting theological differences has past. The time has come to seek overt theological confrontation within the framework of the Christian university. Professional theologians are or ought to be indispensable for these occasions. (A Christian university that does not have professional theologians in its faculty is an odd show indeed.)

But others ought to be drawn into the argument, and not only the crypto-Christians. For too long universities of every sort have put an unwittingly heavy premium on disguised and not just on informal theology; and so a lot of heavy fire has come from concealed positions. No one's true interests are properly served by that.

Chapter Five

REVELATION AND THE VARIETY
OF THEOLOGICAL BELIEFS

I

The theological beliefs upon which I wish to concentrate are those pertaining to Man and to Providence. On these fronts there is already considerable action. The action is not always acknowledged to be theological, but theology is not necessarily enhanced by persuading people that they are already doing it. What I have in mind, then, is to deal largely with theological contentions peculiarly appropriate to the life of the university at the present time.

In speaking of theological beliefs I do not intend that " beliefs " should have a skeptical ring or that the word should serve as a stern theological reproof to the few metaphysical system builders visible in the present philosophical scene. The point is a very modest one: Many people entertain beliefs about Man and about the governance of the cosmos quite apart from a systematic conceptual account of reality. It is an academic commonplace that a systematic conceptual account of reality is a peculiarly feckless enterprise, but this does not mean that people generally have been stripped of all positive convictions about the structures and powers of being least avoidable in the daily round. They may indeed be quite ready to defend these elemental

113

convictions against sophisticated philosophical attack, but they are not likely to believe that these convictions are only popular reductions of the relevant chapters of a grand systematic treatise.

In our time the strife of university faculties is not best understood as a beleaguered philosophy department trying to protect its citadel against its enemies, the outposts having long since been wiped out. In respect to elementary convictions about human nature and the human good every man in the university is likely to be his own philosopher, but this is hardly a serious threat to the integrity and the prospects of philosophy as a departmental operation. Quite to the contrary, actually, this is the age in which professional philosophers stand in line, if necessary, to confess publicly that they have no subject matter of their own. This has not led to wholesale dismantling of philosophy departments and the auctioning of the assets to the highest bidders. Perhaps this is attributable to the fact that the university moves generally with the most commendable caution to put into practice even the most staggeringly apparent material inferences of its own premises.

Again, what philosophy has driven away has found lodging elsewhere. If philosophers find the big questions too formidable or too banal or too cloudy, others are ready to embrace them, even when the issues are clearly theological — when, that is, they have to do with God and man and man's well-being.

So theological beliefs become the explicit content of academic operations in other departments. This is not to say that other departments offer courses designated " Theology " (to say nothing of " Metaphysics ") . At the moment very few departments of religion do such blatant advertising at the undergraduate level. But the content is rather more significant than the designations and advertisements. Not too long ago, for example, we were hearing a good bit about Shakespeare's doctrine of man from academicians who certainly did not consider themselves either philosophers or theologians any more than did sweet Will himself. Tragedy, too, has been an immensely attractive hunting ground for informal theologians, and quite understandably, since theological convictions come to the surface in the great achievements of this kind of art. Indeed our contemporary tragedians would rather have us get the message than revel in the medium if a choice between them were forced upon us.

Historically the wide diffusion of theological beliefs in the university and in society at large was a clear indication of the power and the coherence of the Christian community. Then as now the circumference of the Faith was far greater than the circle of technical and systematic theology. But now the Christian community is no longer socially coherent, and the Faith has been largely reduced to amiable sentiments that provide reinforcement for life-patterns created out of other elements and in response to other powers. What is called Christianity has become a ceremonial decoration on institutional and personal life otherwise determined. Thus in almost every kind of college and university a rich diversity of theological convictions has long existed. The exceptions are schools that are still denominationally parochial. Even there one often encounters a quiet dissent from the dogmatic charter and consensus. True, parochial schools continue to look for orthodox faculty to teach mathematics, astronomy, and biology — especially biology. Often they are forced to settle for competent specialists, who will keep dissenting theological convictions to themselves, or for incompetent persons, who are willing to atone for their academic shortcomings by teaching Sunday school classes and leading prayer meetings.

II

Nevertheless it is more than simple charity to claim that an impulse indispensable to true Christianity survives in this wrongheaded parochialism. The Christian community is not in its distinctive business until it has related all the principal features of human life, in all the peculiarities of local formation, to that truth it calls Revelation. So far then as it is Christian, a university must honor this same obligation. Indeed a Christian center of higher learning has a quite distinctive form of this obligation that derives from its more general obligation to pursue and promulgate the truth by the refinement of the powers of criticism.

Unfortunately the time seems singularly unpropitious for this particular emphasis. That is, the time is *theologically* unpropitious. With the exception, again, of parochial establishments, the Christian colleges are not prepared to honor their obligations, not because they have gone too far down the road of theological pluralism but because the claims of Revelation have been greatly softened by the theologians themselves. An appropriate name for this process is " radical existentializing," so long as we can agree that a particular philosophical movement or *bistro Weltanschauung* is not being made a whipping boy for theological aberrations. In fact the process was well under way before the *Weltanschauung* was bottled for export. The dehydration of Revelation began as a flight from propositional truth to the truth of personal relationship — the truth of Encounter. Thus Revelation is " God speaking," but he does not utter dogmatic propositions. Man, not God, is the creed maker, even though religious men are shrewd enough to point to God as the instigator and accessory. Moreover, to say " God speaks " is to say that *God acts in history:* his " word " is his saving deed. What God does, he does in public, but only the eye of faith recognizes *God* in the doing.

Even so, words are indispensable. Human words, at that. If *propositional* truth-claim is ruled out from any place of honor in Revelation, somewhere close to the throne of grace we must expect to find the word of *testimony*. If it is said that Jesus Christ is God's testimony to himself, to his purpose, his love, then we must expect to say very shortly there-

116

after that some human words are authentic testimony concerning Jesus Christ, e.g., the New Testament. Whatever theory about the miraculous inspiration of that testimony might be forthcoming, it would still be necessary to understand it as we understand testimony in general. That is, we should expect still — perhaps especially here — to distinguish between a conviction proffered as a true account of something and testimony adduced in support of such a conviction. Moreover, we should have to be clear about the intent of the conviction before we could properly manage the testimony. So if a man says that a particular conviction grew out of his reading the New Testament, he has so far offered only a kind of causal explanation of that belief. But if he says he is certain his belief is true, and does not mean by that to disclose how deeply attached he is to it, his appeal to the testimony of the New Testament is clearly an appeal to the shape and movement of life gotten from obedience to Jesus Christ. Otherwise we should have to suppose that the appeal is to convictions held by other people who are felt to be so superior to us that they have a right to tell us what to believe, in perpetuity, even though they have long since died and can therefore have no way of knowing what we might have learned about God and Man since their time.

Ought we then to conclude that we have no access to Jesus Christ save by the meticulous historical reconstruction of his person and his actions? Hardly. From the beginning Christian people have made great metaphysical claims about Jesus Christ. They have, in fact, claimed to have discovered in him the answer to all life's deepest questions and not simply the answer to the question, How we can get through the years of our lives without flying to pieces or flying at each other?

These metaphysical claims cannot be substantiated by any kind of appeal to historical matters of fact, whatever they are. It is conceivable, though not very likely, that we could learn from historical investigation whether Jesus actually rose from the dead. (Many contemporary theologians will ask to be excused from that particular field trip.) But it is not at all conceivable that we could learn from any type of historical investigation whether all men shall rise from the dead. Paul argues that if Christ did not really rise, then there is no hope that we shall; but the argument is framed by a Christian and it is addressed to Christians, which is but to say that the Christian hope of resurrection is grounded absolutely on the resurrection of Jesus Christ as itself the triumphant testimony concerning the specific way God uses his power to achieve his purpose for the transformation of the human enterprise.

Other metaphysical claims concerning Jesus Christ offer less rather than more scope for historical fact-finding, e.g., that he is the being for whom and in whom all things have been created. I do not mean that these ascriptions of power, honor, and glory to Jesus Christ did not grow out of experience of some sort. People do not, as a rule, say things like this unless they have encountered something extraordinary. But there is another and rather different possibility: Jesus Christ threw a very great light upon man's experience of the extraordinary, and this light did not at the time itself seem extraordinary. He " dwelt among us, full of grace and truth; and we esteemed him not." I have, of course, telescoped the Old Testament and the New Testament here, but only to highlight an already striking feature of New Testament testimony, i.e., that God was *incognito* in the man Jesus Christ. The light that he threw upon the human scene, both upon the ordinary and the extraordinary, was itself, in the experience of it, rather more ordinary than world-shattering; until men began to see that he had brought a pattern and a power by which the ordinary and the extraordinary become one world shouting the praise of the one God; began, that is, to see that life and death are not separate domains under separate gods, but are elements of the Kingdom of the everlasting and all-merciful God;

began, that is, to see that the mystery of the existence of a stone is quite as great as the mystery of Orion and of all the morning stars singing on the morning of Creation. Such a light is not the light of Sunday, particularly. It is the light of the daily world, it is the light in which all is done that is done. Such a light is entitled to a day in which we do nothing but sing its praises.

The personalist-existentialistic interpretation of Revelation is so far right, then, in insisting that Revelation is personal, is, in some sense, a Person. But a mistake is made just as soon as this certainty is supposed to cancel another one, i.e., the certainty that verbal testimony must be taken to corroborate theological-metaphysical convictions of the first magnitude of importance. I do not mean that verbal testimony is the only kind available in general and therefore here. But the matter at stake is a verbally expressed belief, a belief that such and such is the case. If a disposition were the object of " proof," testimony beyond the verbal would be called for. If I say that I am well disposed toward someone and do nothing to show that this is the case, my statement may be put down as an empty avowal. But if I say that Jesus Christ is the Lord of History, I can confidently expect to be asked, What have people *said* to confirm such a conviction? as well as, What do you mean by saying it?

A dogma, in this instance a dogma concerning Jesus Christ, is then a metaphysical conviction for which religious warrants are forthcoming. This is one kind of theological proposition. To call such " metaphysical " is to say that such propositions are not to be confused with psychological statements or with statements about history. The religious life of the Christian normally includes all three kinds of statements, to be sure: (1) " I have found peace in the Christ of God "; (2) " Jesus went about doing good "; (3) " In Jesus Christ the fullness of Deity dwelt bodily." All of these have something to do with Revelation. So far as (3) is understood as a metaphysical conviction, it is not a restatement of (1) and (2). Logically it sets the stage for (1) and (2), since it puts into motion, so far as a single proposition could, the whole body of Christian faith. Thus it has the most to do with Revelation since it states the mode of God's presence with man and, therefore, how this God makes himself known to man.

But what has happened to Revelation as the summons from the Eternal God (or Transcendent Being) to the individual to decide for authentic existence? Denied this, or even if this is seriously compromised, much of contemporary campus Christian apologetics evaporates. At this point I am not aiming to produce that result but I am prepared to accept it as an unavoidable implication. Given the Christian account of God, man, and man's place in the world, authentic existence is a grand thing to which to be summoned. Given Revelation, that is, a passion for authentic existence is certainly becoming. But we cannot get that account of reality from authentic existence, and without that account, " authentic existence " becomes another name for man's deadly propensity for taking himself with ultimate seriousness. It is not profitable to be serious about the world, or about one's life, unless one knows what world one is dealing with and what self. Passion cannot endow the world or the self with a value not otherwise discoverable in either.

III

It was suggested above that ideological contentions in the university have two focuses. One of these is Man. The second is Providence.

1. Existentialism is a reminder that Man is an inextirpable theological passion. The delineation of this passion is a variegated operation. So, our task now is to sketch part of the range across which the meaning and value of the passion are pursued. Thereafter we shall seek to determine where Christian convictions fit into this picture.

a. Various kinds of scientific warrant are claimed for the proposition that man is an animal whose distinctive achievements spring from his powers of speech. Once man was admired as the only thinking animal, at least on this planet. Now he is regarded as merely a better thinker than rats and chimps, if we may suppose that the psychologist who builds the maze is really one step ahead of his rats. (On the other hand, the rats are smart enough to make an easy and safe living by playing the psychologist's odd games.) But his superiority in the department of thought is really the same as his superiority in the department of speech. Should one infer that man will lose whatever is left of his vaunted hegemony when a species arrives that can outtalk him, and the magnification of the threats of cancer, termite, staphylococcus, etc., can be written off as hysterical propaganda?

The full stature of this outlook is not achieved until speech is absorbed into a biological-physiological scheme of interpretation. Then man not only is seen to be a product, an effect, of his new environment. He is the result of a particular conditioning given to his biological inheritance.

Developed out to this end, naturalism emerges as a kind of materialism. Philosophers can be counted on to take up arms for or against avowed materialism argued as a metaphysical case. Many people in the university do not follow high-altitude metaphysical debates. Some profess not to understand what is at stake. Others insist that philosophers habitually bog down in merely verbal controversy — " they deal only with words, not with facts." Thus to call an outlook " materialistic " is neither to rebut it nor to reprove its adherents, unless the import of the argument is broadened to encompass concern for the human good. Yet even when that is done, informal theologians and metaphysicians partial to materialism are less intimidated by the specter of inconsistency than are technical theologians and philosophers. Perhaps the dominant concern of informal theology is essentially ethical rather than scientific. Or if " ethical " is too strong, then " practical": totally adequate explanation of human life can hardly matter as much as adequate direction of its energies. So even if a fully and coherently conceptualized materialism stood as the best explanation, a reasonable person might feel that he was not yet clearly instructed as to how he ought to live. Does this go far toward showing that he is not sufficiently rational? The matter is perplexing. Ethical convictions have a habit of going their own way independently of the winds of metaphysical doctrine. Thus a materialist may lament the death of honor even though he believes that man is not really moved by his aspirations. He not only prefers to live one kind of life rather than another, but as a thinking creature he believes that good reasons for his preferences are available. When the reasons are stated he may think ill of them, but his considered judgment that they are poor reasons is hardly a matter of preference or, even less, of impulse.

Are we to conclude from this that people are natively and incorrigibly inclined to accept as valid and good the values of the society which they prefer to all others, whatever their theological convictions? If so, what are we to make now of the vaunted powers of criticism? Are students in ethics courses to learn — at least on purpose — only what kind of language ethical discourse is? Are they to be required to go beyond this and learn what the principal ethical theories are? An ethical theory is a conviction about the human good formulated as a hypothesis. It is a theory, that is, of an exceptional kind: it seeks to account for what man ought to seek rather than for what, in reality, he pursues. It is not a description of his behavior, it is a delineation of what is really normative for the evaluation of human conduct.

Informal theologians may not appear to be edified or instructed by any such business. They will continue to act from certain moral principles, and to support or oppose public policy on the grounds that it is good or bad, right or wrong — and all of this without so much as the hint of a blush for having done something intellectually gauche, viz., pretending that principle and reason can on suitable occasion override any and all conditioning. In fact, informal theologians may very well find themselves at ethical and ideological odds with professional theologians and philosophers, and especially with those who try to soften the harsh reality of normative demands. For what can the nonprofessional moralist make of the proposal that ethics has to do with evaluations of morality rather than with moral prescriptions and injunctions themselves? Or that ethics is simply an analysis of the language in which moral sentiments and judgments are expressed? In becoming modesty the professor of moral philosophy disavows responsibility for telling his students how they ought to behave, except, of course, as members of an academic community. On the other hand, he must have some pretty firm notions concerning the proper conduct of an argument about morals. He must know not only how moral judgment works but also when it is working well. He must know, and be able to show, that if the soundness of Thrasymachus' convictions about the ethical supremacy of might depends upon the arguments Thrasymachus advances, Thrasymachus is wrong. But if Thrasymachus' position is sound independently of his and all other arguments, the professor must be able to show that all other positions are equally sound; and thus that to call an ethical position sound apart from all arguments is to pay it a meaningless compliment.

There is no way of knowing in advance whether philosophical ruminations of this sort will make any appreciable difference to informal theologians and moralists. It is reasonable to expect that they will be considerably more interested in concrete moral convictions and arguments than in logico-dialectical moves. One of the most deeply rooted of such convictions is theological, whether or not it is expressed in conventional religious language. This is the belief in an inclusive ethical community whose demands transcend domestic commitments. Thus a policy or a practice is accused of being a denial of something essentially human. It is not enough to say that it denies something essentially British or something essentially American or something essentially Bantu. More and more voices in the university bespeak the claims of what is really good for man, rather than the rights and privileges bestowed upon particular men by arbitrary statute. This message is not always coherent, but we can hardly doubt or mistake the mounting passion with which it is delivered. For those who credit it no appeal to regional or national self-interest, however highminded, or to the Judeo-Christian tradition, in whatever degree of idealistic evaporation, will suffice. The net of moral commitment must be thrown more widely than the relativizers — so lately in the ideological saddle — could either understand or consent to. The target has again become (or is in a fair way to become) the essentially and (one would hope) the indestructibly human.

The change calls for an elevation of criticism, that is, for a heightening and clarifying of the critical sense. To determine what is ethically compatible with the American ethos certainly calls for a modest outlay of critical acumen. To determine how or whether the American ethos cheapens, distorts, or defeats, the human spirit calls for a far greater critical effort as well as for a world-ranging moral passion. This expanding criticism and passion ought to be matched with a growing clarity of theological conviction.

b. On the informal theological side, then, it is again becoming acceptable, if not *de rigueur,* to espouse belief in Man as an organic spiritual reality underlying and including all expressions of personal and cultural individuality. In the scientific sectors of the university Freud may have the better of it. In the Humanities it is Jung rather than Freud, if and when the issue comes to conscious resolution. And why not? Freud was never able to throw off the "biological bias," or to see any good reason why he should. Jung

124

speaks for the autonomy of the kingdom of spirit, though not very persuasively for its rational superstructures. The spirit is inexhaustibly fecund, and its taproot reaches into the mysterious depths of reality.

I think it quite unlikely that we have yet seen the apogee of this theological conviction, even though specific scientific formulations of it may drop away. For this is an age in which regional loyalties run afoul of mighty economic and scientific forces daily reducing the size of the earth. The Jungian conviction is ready-made, if not heaven-sent, for this situation because it makes the most of an underlying spiritual unity of mankind out of which springs a cultural diversity that is not so diverse as it seems.

The Jungian theology is far more democratic than the long dominant Hegelian theology of culture. Surely we count this a virtue of policy if not of principle. The Jungian outlook does not oblige us to believe that some cultures are nearer to ideal perfection than others. Even if we do privately believe that our society is much higher in the scale of perfection than any other, restraint in advertising this wins prompt and wide approval.

Moreover, the Jungian theology more easily accommodates the American conviction concerning the high value of conscious personal striving. (I do not suppose that Jung can be credited with this; but, again, we are dealing with pervasive informal theologies and not with a specific philosophical-scientific corpus.) The emphasis does not fall upon a providential dialectic that by a fiendishly cunning dialectical process will bring man to fulfillment in history, no matter what this individual or that one does. Even if the creative life should turn out to be a way in which the Collective Unconscious expresses itself, the creative moments cannot be arranged in a dialectical-eschatological progression. Thus the inexhaustible kingdom of the Unconscious functions reflectively much more as the basis of recognition than as a causal explanation of creative attainment. So to recog-

125

nize that all men are brothers is at once to acknowledge a grand common Source, inexpugnably spiritual; and a destination, inalienably human.

c. It is, however, not the case that our world has heard the last of egoism and its theological defense. There are still those who devoutly believe that man is no more real than the individual ego protecting itself from all the inimical powers of the world and aggrandizing itself at the expense of all, if necessary — as it generally is. Miss Ayn Rand, for example, has had a relatively small following on the campuses, but it has been an unusually dedicated one. This primitive form of egoistic individualism may very well be beneath the serious attention of professional philosophers and theologians, but it crops up frequently enough where informal theology is likely to be decisive. It is a theological option for which some people are likely to reach at a moment when the individual seems to be fighting for his spiritual life against the crushing might of superorganizations, even though the images, doctrines, and prescriptions of Miss Rand's individualistic egoism are drenched with Promethean excess. But the enormous success of corporate giantism, whether in business or in politics — both national and international — is easily represented and appropriated as the fruit of a diabolical conspiracy to absorb or extinguish the strong significant individual. So even where the Promethean note misses the mark, the darkly persuasive hints of conspiracy do not; so even lowercase egos who want to be left alone in blissful smallness and anonymity and in that to enjoy fantasies of power and position which do not demand to be translated into conscious drives for either power or place — even these believe that the mighty powers of the Establishment work together as an omniscient machine to render futile the screen of anonymity. When they want you they know where to find you. But they never want you for your own sweet self, rather as raw material for mill or mart or murder.

126

Revelation and the Variety of Theological Beliefs

It is a part of American religiousness to believe that individualism is clearly taught by Judaism and Christianity alike. This is one of the reasons why the " Judeo-Christian tradition " is viewed as the absolute achievement of the spiritual world. This central principle is therefore available as a criterion in appraising the value of specific religions. It is a rusty scythe; but in the interior world it has brought down proud towers of doctrine and liturgy, and in the public world even the high and mighty salute the idol of individualism in passing.

Professional theologians ought to be wary of issuing enthusiastic obituary notices for popular religious and philosophical sentiments. There is little to choose between admitting that Individualism is after all not yet quite dead and being a grudging witness to its resurrection — little of comfort in either choice. For that matter it is not the business of the proper theologian to tell his contemporaries what they believe or to guess how many of them believe this and how many that, or how difficult it really is for them to believe what he tells them they do believe. His business is to propose what might and what ought to be believed and why. There is no virtue in his not knowing what sentiments persist or perhaps prevail in his precincts. Knowing that does not make him a theologian. Not knowing it might make him an unprofitable one.

These considerations have a particular poignancy when theologians are treating the subject of man. Authentic Christianity is good news for the kingdom of man. But suppose that prevailing estimates of human worth are depressing, are indeed so depressing that many many people have appropriated as an anodyne a hopelessly vapid and bland optimism, and fondly look upon it as a first cousin of Christianity — as though Pollyanna, now with a D.D., were a lineal descendant of Jesus Christ. That, a theologian ought to reckon with; but with the whole situation first, that is, with the depressing estimates of human worth and human

127

destiny from which sentimental optimism is as much and truly an escape as the most invariant and immutable catatonic shock.

2. Now let us examine the second focus, Providence. Man is a diverse creature. He seems no more diverse or " diversable " than when he asks, Who am I? and, For what good do I exist? Significant diversity of answer to such questions is quite as likely to appear in the Christian university as elsewhere. Explicit theological confrontation with this diversity will be as difficult and important there as elsewhere. We shall have more to say on that after we have sampled the diversity of conviction concerning Providence.

But first, why Providence rather than God? Surely in any significant synoptic account of the world " God " comes before " Providence." This is what one would suspect in anything called systematic theology; for how shall we speak of God's management of the world until we are sure who God is, or what kind of God actually exists?

So let us say again that we are not dealing here with technical formal theology and metaphysics. In those disciplines " God " surely comes before " Providence." Informal theology is a different picture. There one finds little patience with proofs or disproofs of God's existence and with profound discourses on the Divine Attributes. Other matters seem more pressing. They seem more pressing because they have, or seem to have, a far more direct bearing upon actual value commitments. Thus philosophers are again arguing about the existence and nature of God. In fact they evince much more hardihood in this than the great bulk of contemporary Protestant theologians. But informal theologians are not greatly impressed either by the thirty-six proofs for God's existence lined out by one of America's great philosophers, or by newly formulated proofs of the impossibility of God's existence. Rather, the great question is, How does the good fare at the hands of cosmic powers? This is not to say that the informal theologians are seeking to learn who or what God is from a close inspection of the way in which the great world, the cosmos, is governed. It would be silly to rule out such an interest on a priori or systematic grounds. Where such an interest stirs, one can, of course, assure the person that very little novelty can be found there except in the line of dialectical maneuvers. Informal theologians have a pretty slender confidence in dialectics. Today this general skepticism about any dialectical route to knowledge is triumphantly acclaimed and elevated by the prevailing temper of formal Protestant theology, which is hostile to any dialectical route to knowledge of God. This display of theological negativity is prompted by a religious conviction rather than by a philosophical crotchet: The real nature of the " cosmic government " is not open to religiously neutral inspection, no matter how high-minded it may be. One cannot seriously expect the stone to give the religiously neutral spirit a religiously significant answer to the question, Who made you? No more ought we to expect any imp of excruciating pain or of sordid evil to disclose, to any honest and anguished inquirer, what office in the courts of heaven had given him license to raise hell with so fair and tender a creature as man, and more particularly, with the inquirer's more estimable kinsmen if not with the inquirer himself. The divine government is sued for the greatest sums when the inquirer is his own advocate.

I suppose that many feel a twinge of sympathy for the reactions of the religiously committed when the uncommitted invoke some principle of justice higher than all known gods. An unknown god is perhaps best served by religious neutrality, except when one's own foot is forced into the boot of pain. Then some known and treasured principle is sure to be invoked as the bar before which all other gods are summoned to be asked, Which of you has inflicted this pain upon the fairest of the fair, Man?

Nevertheless, it may be that the question about Divine Providence is not quite the nightmare thing envisaged by so many contemporary theologians. It may be *this* question: Granted that God is thus and so, where are the lines of his administration? Granted that God's " policy commitments " are thus and so, where are we to look to see these being worked out? Are there any reliable indications of the stage in the divine economy to which the world has come and of what impends? I do not suppose that there is any good way of knowing in advance how serious informal theologians are when they say, " Granted that God is such and such." How much of traditional teaching are they assenting to? That is something we cannot know without empirical investigation, and that I cheerfully delegate to the sociologists of religion. There is something we can be reasonably sure of apart from that kind of research. We can be sure that the theological interest of the uncommitted will be seriously engaged when the committed are ready to pursue the value inferences of their own faith in God. " Providence " is the comprehensive category under which these value inferences can be subsumed.

This is to say that the commanding questions concerning God are not those bearing on what God is in himself, to use traditional language. Rather, the prime question is, What is God's concern with the good and how efficacious is that concern? So our next item of business is to sketch the theological options on Providence that enjoy the most commanding position in the university scene.

a. The divine policy is always to reward the righteous and deprive (and perhaps otherwise to punish) the unrighteous. But only God knows who is really righteous and how he means to reward them. We do know that the divine scheme of reward and punishment will not be fully evident until time and the world have come to their divinely appointed end.

This view probably bears the stamp of orthodoxy, in the intellectual scene as well as in popular religious circles.

b. The ultimate cosmic powers are on the side of righteousness. But either we do not know what this righteousness is or we do not understand why Heaven is so patient with wickedness on earth.

How could so weak a view retain any adherents among thinking people? Perhaps because it expresses a residual optimism about the place of the good in the cosmic scheme. And perhaps also because it expresses a residual humility about human familiarity with the divine mind.

c. The main business of the cosmos is the production of moral value. So an outbreak of wickedness in history is no more a breakdown of the cosmic order than is the occurrence of cancer in an innocent child. Accordingly, a person who indicts the cosmos because he hurts somewhere, either for himself or for others, is really a churl — if he were not alive to the presence of value, he could have no complaint. If he says, more modestly, that there is more pain than is necessary, we must ask him how he (or God, for that matter) could know in advance how much pain is necessary? Would he perhaps recommend an overall reduction of sensitivity or of consciousness or of value with a view to reducing the amount and variety of pain? This option has had considerable support from philosophical idealists of theistic bent. It represents an overcoming of the agnosticism evident in b. But this very bravery both in the face of circumspect agnosticism and of hideous immensities of human perversion in this century makes it suspect. Moreover, intellectuals are at the moment acutely discomfited by any proposal to *prove* anything unless it be the obvious.

d. The secret of the universe is that it has no secret. Reality is absurd; the cosmos as such has no " government."

This credo is not so nihilistic as it probably sounds to the elder statesmen who subscribe either to a or to c. Camus, for example, saw in this nonprovidential state of affairs the maximum opportunity for the expression of creative freedom. Delivered from serfdom to divine decrees a man can become what he will, within the limits — whatever they are

131

— of finitude. He need not, and he ought not, blame the conditions of finitude upon some higher intending power.

These theological convictions are encountered in a situation where the generality of people assume that they have an adequate knowledge of God. One hears the deplorable thinness of this knowledge frequently declaimed. But one is stoutly defied to improve upon it or to show that this lean budget of divine truth is inadequate for any of the main purposes of life. The religious situation, in other words, remains vaguely theistic: There is, there must be, a Supreme Being, but he is too great, or his other business is too demanding, or he is too much of a gentleman, to become an intrusive element in the common world.

If we were to round out the view of God involved in this pervasive theism, something like the following would emerge. God is a spiritual power without specific localization. He is committed to the enrichment of the world and he is probably dedicated to helping Man in any way this creature can be helped or needs help, so far as God himself has any resources that he can command for this purpose.

There are, of course, people who profess no interest at all in the question of Providence; and there are the atheists. As for the former we may reasonably expect the group to be diverse. It includes those whose grip upon the good is so strong that the cosmos can be left to take care of its other interests, whatever they are. It also includes those whose grip upon the good is so tenuous that they wish not to raise any issues which would weaken that grip even further. The atheists, on the other hand, certainly do not offer uniform opposition to Providence. Doctrinaire Marxists, for instance, have a superb confidence in the outcome of history. They make an interesting contrast to Christian thinkers who do not believe that history as such has any meaning or that Revelation has anything to say about the government of the cosmos. I shall not develop this contrast, because we have agreed not to concentrate upon the upper levels of conceptual clarity and ideological definiteness. We are concerned with root theological convictions rather than with systematization and dialectics. Our hope in this is to delineate a particular responsibility of the Christian college in our time. *This is the responsibility to bring root theological convictions into the kind of sharpness of formulation that will make the moral implications of these convictions unmistakable.*

IV

One need not look far to find religious conviction and commitment in this delineation of responsibility. What remains is to sketch the principal features of this religious stance.

1. Acceptance of the revelation of God in Jesus Christ is an acceptance of a way of knowing God that is normative for all other knowledge of God.

2. Acceptance of the revelation in Jesus Christ is an acceptance of a way of serving God that is normative for all other ways of serving God.

3. The connection between knowing God and properly serving him is so terribly close and demanding that apart from divine grace we could not endure it.

When these things are taken together, the practice of the Christian life assumes paramount importance for both informal and formal theology. Both modes of theology may persist in ignoring the Christian life, or in cheapening it, but that is another matter. To put the claim as strongly as possible, it is in the practice of the Christian life that the God who is the Father of Jesus Christ makes himself known. For wherever Christ is acknowledged and honored as Lord, some obligation is felt to practice the life of love as he commanded. I say " some obligation " to emphasize the matter of boundaries: How far is that love to extend? Can any person or any segment of the body of mankind be left out deliberately, with Christian purpose? If so, what is that purpose that we may invoke the name and authority of Christ to hallow it? These are desperately difficult questions, no doubt. But the fundamental difficulty is not abstract or conceptual. It is the difficulty of practicing, concretely, the community of all mankind. Who would follow Christ must do more than posit and admire that community as a noble, perhaps the noblest, idea. That community *is* an ideal, an objective, a criterion. But it is also the place, the context, of God's self-disclosing action. Thus "Christ" is the proper name of a community. We may endow it with ideal features and even with a romantic aura, but it is as bluntly actual as my obstreperous neighbor and as brutally demanding as the cross.

So in the Christian faith the revelation of God in Jesus Christ stands forth as the disclosure of the shape, the form, of the real world. This form is given as something already there, that is, as fully actual. It is also an obligation binding upon my powers of enactment. It is something seen and something to be done.

This is why the Christian must be prepared to argue about the shape of the real world. For him religion is a "reality game" as well as an ethical command, and it is neither to the exclusion of the other. But in his arguments with other theological options he cannot surrender his primordial acknowledgment of Jesus Christ as the being in whom the real shape of the world is disclosed. If he gives up there, he has given up the distinctive substance of Christianity. This is what is properly meant by the primacy of Revelation in the argument and life of a faithful Christian.

I have already paid my respects to the view of the rational man as the one who approaches every issue with an open mind, but I cannot forgo the opportunity to say again that this view strikes me as a very remarkable confusion of a principle of criticism with a real life-option. To live humanly is to have and to express a personal order of value that is only in part a construction of reason, even though the whole of it may be open to rational criticism. There is no a priori assurance that even the most rational part of any life-option can handle reality's traffic. Such assurance as is forthcoming is available only in an empirical community, much of which derives from nonrational powers. So the scientist acknowledges the scientific community. So the religious man acknowledges the church.

V

I have not attempted even to suggest how Christians, whether they be formal or informal theologians, ought to argue the case for Christianity against other options. Here I have contended that the Christian university is a natural context in which to make that case. The revelation of God in Jesus Christ ought not to be construed as a license to create special provinces of intellect and aspiration into which only a select minority can enter. Faith in Jesus Christ ought, rather, to endow one with an unshakable confidence in the unity of all mankind in the creative and redemptive love of God.

There are great mysteries in this. We are surrounded by them. We are penetrated by them to the marrow. But it is not *theological* business to invoke them, and it is a theological impropriety to flee to them for cover when anti-Christian artillery fire becomes accurate as well as deafening. The world is not lost when we lose an argument. Souls may not be saved when we win arguments. No matter: the Lord is to be served with every power of spirit and word, and right joyfully, at that.

So in theological argument in the university the Christian claims neither privileged knowledge nor dialectical immunity. He does, of course, claim to have grasped the import of the human story but he does not have this as a private treasure of mind and heart. He has it only so far as he is ready to enact it. This enactment is the practice of Christian community. And this is, veritably, the love of God.

Chapter Six

THE COLLEGE CHAPEL:
A VIBRANT FRAGMENT OF THE CHURCH

I

If we begin by speaking of a fragment, we must have in mind a whole. Very well. In this case the whole is the church. The fragment of particular concern here is the college chapel, but to call it a fragment is already to beg a question. Or if not that, it is to be presumptuous, nonetheless, for the college chapel often seems more attractive, more plausible, and more relevant than the traditional church across the street. It may well have better preachers than the churches on the perimeter of the campus. It is almost certain to have better music. The congregation has more literate people in it. The prophetic voices of the hour are more likely to be heard in the chapel.

But is the chapel really a church? If we are to deal fairly with this persistent question, we must see what lies behind it as theological prepossession about the Christian church. This is a formidable undertaking in a time when the best theological minds are wrestling once again with ecclesiological issues of the highest import, in response both to the rising tide of ecumenism and to parochial pressures.

The present occasion does not permit an extensive excursion into such profound matters. Instead I shall give a very brief digest of what traditional Christianity has taught concerning the church. Then I shall ask whether the university chapel is more than a fragment of that. This procedure ought not to prejudice the possibility that if the chapel *is* a fragment, that particular fragment is more vibrant and more luminous than the putative whole.

The traditional teaching is that the church is a community created by the direct action of God and blessed by the uninterrupted presence of God in it until the end of the world. God willed from the beginning that this community should proclaim and body forth the Kingdom of Jesus Christ, manifesting the divine righteousness and all other perfections of the Kingdom, save its world-consuming glory, in every natural and supernatural manner of communication available to it. He has never changed his mind about this. Therefore, from time to time (if not continuously), he has given freely of his own life for the renewal of the church. The churchly office of prophecy still exists as the peculiar channel through which the demand and the power for renewal are communicated.

From this account of the church one can see why present-day theologians often speak of the church as having " intentional " being. The church exists to carry out the purpose of God to publish his Kingdom to all mankind. In principle none of its forms, functions, and qualities refers to anything else, none of them has or needs any other justification.

My interest in putting the matter so severely has nothing to do with historical primitivism. I do not know whether, in the first moments of its life, the actual church fully sustained this theological description. Many exemplary Christians do believe this, and do believe that the church has ever done so since. Such a belief is beyond historical verification in any ordinary sense, but some who profess it would be content to have it stand as an expression of loyalty rather than as a claim made upon verifiable history. For my part I do not believe that the living church is bound either to adore

137

or to emulate such a historical model, even if such has ever existed. We ought rather to be concerned with the way in which the nature of the church functions as a criterion in its own judgments of itself, here and now. I mean, of course, theological judgment. We are not concerned with the popularity of the church. At the moment we are not even interested in its chances for survival in an age widely and enthusiastically advertised as post-Christian.

II

One kind of theological judgment is discernible in the question, Where is the church? The theologically minded are not likely to be satisfied with the answer, " The church is on the corner of Elm and College." The *Where* question is not geographical. It is a question about unique spiritual condition and unique spiritual function. Thus some contemporary prophets say that the church can be found on the most exposed shore of the Slough of Existential Despair (not to be confused with despondency, which is merely psychological) . Other prophets claim that the church lies at the end of a long hike beyond the last stop of the Streetcar named Desire, at the intersection of Irrelevancy Boulevard and Implausibility Avenue. But prophecy is only one mode of theological judgment. It is the most colorful mode, no doubt, and perhaps it is the most popular in college pulpits. It is also the mode that in our time is the most susceptible to the confusion of spiritual freedom with personal eccentricity and rhetorical flair.

The question, Where is the church? may be taken in a very different way. It may be a call for the delineation of those offices the performance of which is a just and Christianly authentic basis for saying, *Here* is the church. This is the answer I shall now attempt briefly to develop. This attempt may incite the displeasure of persons who suppose that the church exists wherever a certain spiritual condition is found, such as love or otherworldliness or serenity. I do

not believe that any definition or description of the spiritual
life is a theological substitute for a delineation of the church
in terms of its offices. The offices do not, of course, account
for everything. I cannot imagine that there has been a time
when a delineation of these functions was more greatly
needed, nor a time when the mind-set of so many spiritually
sensitive people was more vehemently anti-institutional.
This is part of the vibrancy of the college chapel. It seems
to be a ringing vote against the ecclesiastical Establishment
— and perhaps against the Establishment as such.

1. The first of the offices of the church is *preaching*. (We
are speaking theologically rather than historically. Even so,
our " first " is not to be taken as an indication of importance
relative to the other offices.) The gospel in and of Jesus
Christ is the content of this preaching. The gospel is the
New Testament representation of God, Man, and the di-
vine-human community. On the basis of this representation
a budget of religious and moral prescriptions is composed.
The budget is not uniform in its details from one age to
the next or from one culture to another. But the key elements in it are uniform and for that reason cannot be identified, without critical remainder, with any concrete moral
order or system of morals. Thus the key elements are directives rather than laws, policies rather than conventions.
The church exists wherever this gospel is preached and
heard in the spirit of obedience to a living Lord rather
than to any extant system of morals or to any idealistic program.

Preaching covers a multitude of sins. The sins of the
preaching office of the chapel are our particular interest.
Here we have an interesting spread running from the most
self-righteous trumpeting of the preacher's opinions on the
immoralities of the national government to the most stub-
bornly entrenched concealment of the preacher's opinions
behind the opinions of others, ranging from Paul to Wil-
liam Faulkner, a distance I seem to find rather more con-

siderable than others do. But the church is still present so long as the perpetration of any of these sins generates bad conscience in the preacher and uneasiness in the congregation. It is transparent arrogance on my part to pronounce these practices to be sins against the authentic office of preaching. My intention in such a high-handed performance is not to drive others to their knees in contrition long overdue. It is much more modest. What I conceive to be at stake here is the proper modality in which the gospel is to be preached.

Given the gospel itself, the fundamental modality for its proclamation is declarative and indicative. It is not argumentative nor subjunctive. There is much over which to argue in the theological expansion of the gospel. Argument over doctrinal expansion must be clearly distinguished from argument over the root convictions of faith in the revelation of God in Jesus Christ. It pertains to the preaching office of the church to delineate these root convictions as vividly and persuasively as possible, and to insist that one either believes them to be true and binding or one does not. This is the elementary Either-Or of gospel proclamation. In respect to the psychology of the Christian there is a good bit of coming and going in the faith, even of the most loyally devout. The inner sense of " assurance " rises and falls in response to all manner of temperamental and situational factors. The saints of every persuasion have candidly testified to this. But this does not mean that the root convictions generated by New Testament representations are accordingly to be softened or diluted in order to make them conform to temperamental or situational pressures. It is not possible to be seriously religious if one makes the first religious question, What does temperament or situation demand or permit? The elementary and decisive religious thrust is already an *evaluation* of temperament and circumstance. So the primary modality of expression of all serious religiousness is declarative and indicative rather than suppositional, argumentative (dialectical) , or subjunctive.

This is not to deny that there is a place for one kind of subjunctive in the preaching of the gospel: irony. I for one should like to hear more of this in the pulpit. It would be a welcome seasoning for the preternatural self-seriousness of so much existentialized preaching. Be that as it may, once the fundamental posture of preaching is infected by the subjunctive of contrary to fact, or by the optative subjunctive (" Would that it were true! ") , the gospel has been nullified, so far as human confusion and irresolution can do that.

All of us in the academic community, whatever the stripe of our individual religious commitment, can sense the pathos of the college chapel where the preaching office of the church is at stake. The pathos deepens as the college becomes a university and drifts farther and farther away from whatever formal ecclesiastical ties it once had. Part of the constitutive natural piety of the academic community is a very deep conviction that the college years are or ought to be the time of maximum detachment from all given commitments in the interest of the most searching inquiry into which of them, if any, merits continuance. The preaching of the gospel, if it be heard at all, is almost certain to be treated to this same detachment if not to worse. There are days and days when the college preacher, native or import, can expect to receive the response of Agrippa to Paul: " How interesting — I must hear you again sometime on such matters! "

This natural piety of the college has several dubious features. One is the fact that the call for maximum personal detachment comes at the time when the need and the power of loyalty are psychologically at their peak. It is the time when the need to belong often reaches its most creative, and not just its most spontaneous, expression, precisely because the individual's powers of expression are attaining maximum thrust. How odd, therefore, that just at this age the college student should receive the heady and stern counsel to put all of his commitments to the test, except the commitment to " free inquiry." This counsel and the atmosphere it helps to define are frequently misunderstood. One must have firm ground underfoot to carry on the business of inquiry. Moreover, all inquiry proceeds under the canopy of broad assumptions and attitudes that function as axioms. The " ground condition " is not adequately fulfilled by the general and generous acknowledgment that one is human: one is human in a particular way and in a particular situation. Descartes may have fancied that he had adequate theoretical reasons for not being sure who he was or where he was in space and time until inquiry had pegged these items past all possibility of uprooting. But if he had been actually (shall we say existentially) unsure of these ground conditions, there would have been no theoretical problem, there would have been nothing to explain or to justify. And so of all of us. " Detachment " cannot be taken to mean the dissolution of *all* commitments and acknowledgments, until one finds the magic bond that emerges as solid gold in the vat in which the acids of doubt boil and bubble. We cannot expect our friends to accept blank checks from us until we have put all their credentials and testimony to the test of neutral inquiry. Indeed, one of life's most inevitable and terrible moments is that in which a person discovers in himself and in others a talent for perfidy, if not for treason, and yet will not and cannot dissolve the bonds. There are, that is, loyalties that are the presupposition of perfidy, the necessary condition of treason. The function of inquiry, relative to these ground conditions, must be that of clarification of one's own being in relation to them, and a sharpening of one's powers of discrimination to detect spurious inferences drawn from these ground conditions.

We owe it to ourselves to call attention in passing to another element of pathos in the natural piety of the university. I refer to the demands spreading out from the " therapy of reason," for which alone the university initially accepts responsibility. The university begins by saying: " We will teach you how to think, but someone else must help you take care of your soul." To put it somewhat pretentiously, this is the historical dialectical antithesis of the church college which began by saying: " We will provide nurture for your soul, but we abjure you to refrain from dangerous thoughts." Now the university offers treatment for the whole person. In doing so, we ought to acknowledge that the therapy of reason plays a very large role in the disruption of the soul of the student. The psychiatrists in the department of university health will continue to track emotional illness — soul disruption — into the lair of the home and even farther back into the mother's womb (and I do not know, except metaphysically, how much farther back the inquiry into ground conditions could be pressed). They may not have time to do this with any given student. Nonetheless, the scientific posture is there, and it is part of the therapy of reason in which the university has now a very heavy investment. There is an astonishingly large amount of scientific conventionality in all such therapies, wherever they are applied. In the university they help to conceal the role of the university in disrupting the life of the student. It is not hard to find justification for this upheaval. Why should we *not* candidly say that the college years constitute a rite of passage? Such rites are often painful. That is part of their teleology. Indeed, they are quite certain to be painful if the young person is to get on with creating a new and higher synthesis of the elements of his psyche and his society.

This is not a legitimate warrant for saying the further thing, namely, that the university as such provides a stable structure of commitment to serve as the ground and the canopy for that synthesis which is the end of the rite of passage. In fact, patterns of association spring up in and around the university that have nothing of essential connection with the therapy of reason, such as fraternities, athletics, etc. Moreover, the faculty is not hired to provide such a struc-

143

ture and it is not predictably a paradigm of the rational life. The faculty may indeed include, though its policies are certainly not designed to create, heroes of reason who may also be taken to be models of detachment. It is probably wise to worship these heroes and models from afar. Close inspection is likely to reveal that they are exemplary husbands and fathers (more likely the former than the latter), Freemasons, Kiwanians, and vestrymen; and all of this and more too without apology or excuse. Nietzsche, in the last quarter of the nineteenth century, was mortally afraid that scientific reason was making eunuchs of men. It was undercutting and vitiating the passional nature. I would not for a moment doubt the element of prescience in Nietzsche's violent anxieties. As a satisfactory diagnosis of our own situation it falls very wide of the mark. We do not suffer from a paralysis of the powers of commitment. But we may profitably wonder whether these powers are being dispersed even unto triviality over a broad spectrum of interests and demands. We may also wonder how this dispersal answers to the pressures created by a genuinely critical reason. Once upon a time these pressures were very widely held to be the immanent life of cosmic Reason, in whose perfection all things cohere. This theological conviction has very few subscribers in the contemporary scene.

And yet the university is being driven to pose as omnicompetent in human affairs. It has become the great brainpower reservoir for public administration. Without it the country could not be adequately defended, tilled, fed, amused, or watered. The country at large does not know whether any of its religions or its diversions or its creative expressions are sound and good until the *real* critics, the savants of the university, have spoken. Have spoken and have been translated by popularizers. And while all of this has been going on, has been going from strength to strength, the university has been receding from coherence at a velocity exceeded only by the speed of light.

Moreover, for every hero of reason who has dissolved or refused a major commitment on the grounds of its essential irrationality, there are forty (I speak Scripturally rather than sociologically) who have done so because of alienation of affections or because they feel that Modernity is a comprehensive intellectual and attitudinal system from which they could not escape even if they wanted to. Even the Knights of Reason find themselves obliged to honor commitments about which they have many ethical reservations as well as theoretical doubts, simply because there is no actual escape from the ground conditions of our common life. Most of us, for example, are prepared to sacrifice comfort, career, and even life itself in defense of the nation, whatever doubts we have about the policies that make all of this necessary. Here our preferences and our choices are bounded by irreversible decisions. Yet many of us hesitate, and others decline without hesitation, to make any pledge of commitment to any specific religious community on the grounds that we find its particularity offensive, however edifying its moral aspirations, and we long for a way of being religious that would embrace all the options at once and give us a cool faith without the sweat of embarrassment or sacrifice. We have become so obsessed with the pluralities of the religious life that we are very poorly prepared to acknowledge anything holy in the ground conditions of our existence. Cultural relativism drives us downward into a tribal religiousness: the random boundaries of social existence become divine, that is immutable and absolute, but in nothing holy, that is worthy of adoration rather than of mere acknowledgment.

In this situation the preaching of the gospel is a grave offense. The gospel is a call for a commitment that is both particular and unreserved. It is a call that presupposes an acknowledgment of the holy as the ultimate ground condition. It is a call that elevates the human community as an object of sacrificial love above every idealistic projection of contemporary culture. We can understand, therefore, why college preachers covet theological encouragement to preach something else. We can understand why the substitutes are so appealing to people in the university.

None of these substitutes seems to be so appealing at the moment as a " religionless " faith, preferably one endorsed by a formidable theologian such as Tillich. After all what is the harm in supposing that man is natively and inextirpably religious if this means that we are always and necessarily taking one thing or another with ultimate seriousness? Thus surveyed, the human enterprise, both in its vast sociocultural creations and in the life of the individual, emerges as religious. (Indeed, life itself, and not merely human life, is religious, since all forms thereof persist in being so long as possible.) Particular religions are accordingly historically conditioned symbol systems in which ultimate valuations are expressed, and there are as many ways of being religious as there are ways of finding or investing value in any element of the world.

To tie this generous estimate of the human situation into the best elements of historical Christianity calls for a minimum of theological effort. If we take the vision of the good life as the best element of Christianity, and thereafter reduce that vision to the praise of ethical love, Christianity emerges as the supreme expression — to date — of the agapeistic life. The metaphysical dross of Christianity drops away, miraculously. Therewith much of the scandal disappears, both the theological-historical scandal and the scandal of a legalistic moralism.

Equipped with this theological package, the college preacher is free to summon his constituency to a life of high moral adventure, a supreme commitment to the ideal good. Historical forms of the religious life, such as ecclesiastical organization, dogma, and sacrament, are of value just so far as they symbolize and serve the ideal good. None of them is acknowledged to have a direct bearing on the ground conditions of human life. Overhead is the canopy of ethical aspiration, a firmament in which every high envisagement of the good twinkles amiably, each having escaped its earthy matrix by the same miraculous stroke by which Christian love is freed from the integuments of creed and ceremony.

I do not profess to know whether the university ministry can or would command the resources to meet this dissolution of the Christian gospel. It is indeed far from clear that the university ministry would agree that we are confronted by the dissolution of the gospel rather than blessed with a program for modernizing the essentials of the gospel. I am convinced that this kind of religious amiability is a most unpromising atmosphere for rigorous theological argument. I do not believe that it clarifies or enriches the understanding of either the essential thrust or the diverse particularities of concrete religious communities. It dissolves root ontological convictions into ethical aspirations and relativizes the criteria of ethical aspirations by anointing them with " freedom," " openness," and " flexibility." Furthermore the high celebrative life of any religion is divested, in principle, of any content or reference except ethical aspiration and/or the need for aesthetic self-expression. It is hardly a coincidence that this posture of religious amiability is so compatible with ethical views that put a heavy premium on freedom and a very small bounty on responsibility.

2. The second principal office of the church is the *priesthood*. Before we consider dilutions and corruptions of this office of the church, it will be well to review the prime elements of this ministry of the church.

a. The first element of the priestly office is sacramental. It is the administration of the sacraments as expressions, vehicles, and symbols of the grace of the living God, in that order. A sacrament begins (our theme is Christian history) as the manifest action of God in the human situation. A sacrament is something God does and does directly. It is therefore the sign of God's presence. Thereafter and therefore the sacrament becomes a vehicle of God's grace, a channel through which the power of divine love flows from its irreducibly mysterious source into the human subject. The sacrament is a dramatic enactment in which God's power is resident. It is a form to which God has made a commitment of his own being. It is therefore a place (one could as well say a moment) in which God is uniquely present. It is an occasion in which God's caring for his creaturely image is made uniquely vivid.

Thus sacraments are both celebrative and commemorative. They summon the faithful to an actual participation in the divine life. They commemorate the miraculous moment in which God could be enumerated as one of those present and will be again.

Then the sacrament becomes symbolic: it expresses a visible similitude between the action of God and the action of man, and it assumes a real identity. A sacrament that has become a symbol is no longer able to convey the power of that identity. So it becomes an emblem of the religious community, and affective values accrue to it that owe very little to the original intentionality of the sacrament.

The Christian sacraments have traveled this route. This does not mean that the expressive and transmissive power of sacrament has been irretrievably lost — lost by the operation of a law of the religious life. As God lives he continues to act sacramentally. That I believe to be a prime Christian conviction. But it is also true that the hunger for a religio-cultural synthesis is very acute in this creature we call modern man. When sacraments have reached the symbolic stage they are available for synthesis with elements and powers of culture that have a nonreligious origin and meaning. Thus today the sacramental life of the church is widely accepted even in the church as an archaic symbolization of human values. The ultimate affirmation of the human community in Jesus Christ is thus obscured by a radical anthropocentrism that infects the entire visible life of the church, and nowhere more potently than in the university chapel.

In the face of this process — and probably well before it has reached its greatest triumphs — I am constrained to say that the church exists in even a semblance of wholeness and therefore of authenticity only where the sacraments are celebrated as expressions and vehicles of the grace of God. I do not believe that this is personal eccentricity, a dubious love for medieval stained glass and a cathedral stillness broken only by Gregorian chants. The Christian church persists where living souls find grace to behold God acting sacramentally here and now and everlastingly.

b. The second element of the priestly office is the pastoral. The church of the priesthood is charged with the " care of souls " and it is charged to care for them as no other institution is. This is part of what is confessed as the apostolic life of the church.

The ways in which the church through the ages has made provisions for the body as well as for the soul is itself a deep and proper expression of her spiritual responsibilities. It would be flattering to suppose that Christians have consistently been the most highly sensitized to the sufferings of others. History tells us that this sensitivity has commonly been rather selective. So the church at any moment has much to repent of. But the church does not need to repent or apologize for dedication to a principle of human unity that is at once thoroughly spiritual and concrete. In the light of this principle the church preaches that men ought to be able to exert a moral control over their " members," i.e., over bodily energies. The goal in this is not control for control's sake — a goal sufficiently ego-referencing. The goal is control for the sake of the " upbuilding of the whole community." Creativity, rather than a display of ego strength, is the grand objective of the discipline imposed upon bodily energies by the spirit. But people cannot be expected to acquire this if their bodies are ill, undernourished, or in bondage to the will of others.

149

The pastoral concern of the church has other dimensions as well. The church still plays a significant part in the arrival and departure of human life. The church still has a hand in the elemental and ultimate rites of passage. The real sacramental character of these rites has now been largely obscured in the Protestant world. Baptism has become a pretty ceremony that people attend primarily to watch the antics of the babies. As for the high-contracting parties of the second part, the parents, they embrace the rite of Baptism as the first public occasion for announcing the name of the newborn. Baptism is baby's first nice coming-out party, and it is cheaper than a party at home.

It is hard not to be even more cynical about the pastoral care of the dying and the dead. The Catholics have a stranglehold on Extreme Unction. Protestants have contrived metaphysical excuses for permitting them to enjoy this sacramental monopoly. But what *do* Protestants believe in here? A cheery " so long and good luck " to the dying? Should we offer them congratulations for their having this chance to get to heaven before the rest of us? Mostly we sit in silent agony at the bedside of the dying and hope to recoup at the funeral. But the funeral has nothing of the sacramental about it. It is now a " service " that the undertaker has been thoughtful enough to provide and it is now held in his memorial chapel — a place in which not even the corpse is sure death is real.

The church's disarray in its sacramental life is the opportunity of the college chapel. The attenuation of the sacramental life of the church off the campus has made it possible for some of its symbolism to be employed in the college chapel. Since we shall have more to say about this presently, we shall say nothing more on it at the moment. We turn instead to another aspect of the pastoral office.

The pastoral office of the chapel is now very widely interpreted as that of counseling and of counseling across a wide range of situational crises and emotional disturbances.

150

(This is the case beyond the campus too, but our concern is the campus chapel.) Much of this pastoral counseling is as broad-gauged as the range of problems submitted to it, which is to say that the pastoral counselor draws upon training and principles related to the Christian gospel only by civil marriage, so to speak. It would be unrealistic to expect anything else, given the wide diversity of religious background and expectation which his clients bring with them. But bear in mind also that the pastoral counselor himself has found that he needs considerably more working capital than the gospel seems to provide. He needs technical skills as well as a loving heart and a patient spirit. He also needs to know what is now known about the psyche that was not known by our grandfathers. The faith of our fathers may be living still, but we cannot be good pastors if we turn our backs on the fact that they suppressed their hatred of their own fathers.

Here the Protestant chaplain is prone to think of his situation as vastly superior to that of his Catholic colleague, who, after all, as priest is tightly bound to the canonical manual of moral theology. The priest of the Catholic Church is ecclesiastically authorized to forgive sins, according to a formula over which he has little freedom of revision. The Protestant pastor can forgive sin and use various techniques to uncover the etiology of the unsatisfactory performance. He may even relieve the customer of his sense of guilt, either by explaining why he feels guilty, or by persuading him to adopt his (the pastor's) own moral outlook. In any case he will probably not imbue catharsis and the works of repentance with any explicit sacramental value. I suspect, in fact, that the counselee comes away from many pastoral exposures believing that the worst thing about sin is guilt feeling. Perhaps there is nothing really bad except these negative effects. Given the thinly disguised hedonism of so much freedom talk, why should we doubt it?

We should have no trouble, then, seeing why the college

pastor might easily feel that his counseling is a legitimate and authentic expression of the pastoral office of the church, and that this ministry is rather more intelligently and authentically carried out in the college chapel than in the ordinary church.

So we may begin to wonder how fair it is to speak of the chapel as being a fragment of the church when there is ground for supposing that at least two of the priestly offices are better executed on the campus than they are off of it. Let us then reflect a bit further on the execution of these two offices in the college chapel.

As for the sacraments, we should expect some variations here. Some religious ceremonies occur frequently in the chapel, particularly marriage and the memorial service. Baptism must run a fairly poor third, and the Lord's Supper an even more distant fourth. This order of descending probability and plausibility of occurrence is a testimony to the fact that the Lord's Supper still has about it something of its primordial sacramental character. Moreover, it has far less civil and secular adaptability. It stands out as a peculiarly offensive survival of ancient superstitions. It is, in fact, the scandal of the gospel enacted in the chancel. The church does not run a graver danger of actually being the church than in the celebration of this Sacrament.

The practices of college chapels vary considerably in the observance of the Lord's Supper. On some campuses the denominations have little eucharistic picnics for their elect, often tucked away in dim recesses of unconsecrated buildings. On others the college chapel itself observes Communion at periodic intervals and as a second feature after the main service. High churchmen often ask by what authority this is done. If the question is asked out of ecclesiastical arrogance, it hardly deserves answer. If it is asked out of concern over the reality of the congregation in and for whom the Lord's Supper is celebrated, the question is as meritorious as it is difficult. What is at stake, in other words, is not so much the legitimacy of the orders of the priest as the unity of the congregation in the service of God and loyalty to Jesus Christ. The Sacrament is *ex opere operata* only and precisely to the degree in which the community participates in it, for it is an expression of the community in Christ. A significant portion of the Sunday congregation in college chapels is made up of onlookers. Others attend when the speaker is a person of note, which hardly puts them outside the category of onlooker. Add to this the fact that many college chapels do not advertise themselves as being full-fledged churches and accordingly open their ranks to associate membership. So to what does one commit oneself in accepting associate membership? What rite of passage dramatizes this event? What is the cost? What is the privilege? What are the burdens? What is the reward?

These questions do not spring either from skepticism or from the failure of charity. Rather they express the conviction that the issue of the wholeness of the church is bound up indissolubly with the question of the unity and vocation of the congregation. Put so, we may find the principle of rational detachment more acutely embarrassing than we have yet supposed, to say nothing of such issues as the official religious neutrality of the university administration.

We have already suggested that the conversion of the pastoral office into counseling service, in the church at large, may well make it easier for the college chapel to discharge the pastoral office on the campus than a more traditional reading of that office would allow. The care of souls no longer includes, in any easily recognizable form, a minute inspection of the spiritual condition of the charge, or a spiritual regimen prescribed to strengthen the weak and to tame the unruly. The campus ministry is exposed to the full round of emotional disorders and stresses besetting the students, and their counseling services are by no means limited to the Christian constituency in the student body. On many

153

campuses the chapel ministers see more students on more problems than do the medical and administrative counselors combined. Something rather more than the normal distance separating postadolescence from the parental generation appears to have opened between students and administration, and there are still many students who avoid professional psychiatric counseling for as long as possible. Thus much of the schoolday time of the campus minister is spent in listening to student problems, many of which have no ostensible religious dimension. Thus it has come about that the college minister is called upon, often in tones of sheerest anguish, to offer absolution for sins to persons who reject the category of Sin and are quite sure that God does not exist. Perhaps this is anomalous, but there it is. Anomalous because the university, if not the small church-related college, is well staffed with persons committed to guilt reduction; ranging from the psychologists, who give a scientific causal explanation of guilt feelings; through the psychiatrists, who inflate scientific hypotheses into metaphysical dogmas; to the professors and their disciples, who lead vivid exhilarating lives well beyond the frontiers of conventional good and evil — and whose diaries, submitted in evidence in court trials, read very much like their scholarly bibliographies. Yet the guilty grow from more to more, and suffer great mischief, and too often turn to destruction unless they can wrest absolution from some agent or vehicle of grace. Sensitized to suffering by nature and sometimes by grace, the college minister who turned a deaf ear to this would find himself the grossest self-contradiction.

But what has he to tell the undiscriminating guilty, what has he to tell them that springs from the gospel and from the silently ministering congregation? They have not come to him out of recognition of what he is and for whom he speaks. They have come because they are desperate and they see him as one of the less threatening resources of the college. Characteristically he does not include in his counsel instructions concerning the spiritual life. Indeed he may very well hesitate to express any judgment about their conduct. He may himself have been led to believe that every crisis in the history of the psyche is generated by an emotional illness and therefore he may be very reluctant to reach for such formidable categories as Responsibility and Self-determination, in any case. The last thing he is likely to be tempted to say to the distressed student is, Let us pray, unless the student is on his deathbed and is therefore in no position to file either an injunction or an appeal.

Thus simply by being on hand as one ideologically committed to minister to suffering, the college pastor today is picking up many of the pieces being dropped by faculty personnel in volume tantamount to a blizzard. The advancement of technical scholarship does not predictably coincide with the task of forming and nurturing the minds of the young, but it has even less to do with the care of souls. So the college is rapidly ceasing to be alma *mater*. Through the services of the chapel, through the offices of that fragment of the church, the college may emerge as substitute father. There is hardly anything certain about this, however. The university may weld together the two structures of a degree factory for the unregenerate masses and a high-powered esoteric self-adoring think-center upon which the student masses, the great unwashed, look in holy awe from a great distance, and hurry home to read all about the superluminaries, in *Life*.

I admit to having the gravest apprehensions for both the university and the church, given the unchecked acceleration of such tendencies. The university has no clear right to draw the ministry into a role that is the equivalent of morale officer on an aircraft carrier. The chapel has no religious warrant for serving as the dressing station for the casualties of the university. The church has something to say about sin and about its forgiveness. This is simply not available to anyone who claims that he is sorry for his misdeeds, especially now that he has been caught out. As matters now stand people are quick to believe that God is all-welcoming tender forgiveness and that his whole righteousness consists of this. This view has the singular merit of combining a radical error about God and a grievous misconception of moral responsibility. That churchmen do sometimes commend the view may give it prestige, but prestige is a poor substitute for truth.

What the church has to say about sin and forgiveness is part of an organic account of the world in which human life and the human person come to be as expressions of Almighty God. Before the church becomes a dispenser of comfort to the afflicted it must first be a teller of this truth. This does not mean that the faithful are enjoined to stuff a religious tract into the hands of the sufferer before ministering to his hurt. It does mean that the church in all its agencies, no matter how far-flung, is peculiarly equipped to deal with some kinds of suffering, or with some dimensions of suffering, rather than with all. In default of other angels of mercy the church must of course step in — there is not likely to be a surplus of elemental kindness in the world or on the campus. But for the church to do what others ought to be doing is a poor thing in the long run if they are thereby encouraged to default indefinitely.

3. The third office of the church is *teacher of the truth about God*. The nature as well as the content of this truth is so remarkable that the people of the church frequently betray the liveliest uncertainty and the deepest misgivings about proclaiming it. Perhaps this is why they seem often to be looking for some way to dilute this message and thus make the Christian life more attractive to the passerby as well as easier on the home folks.

One of the most popular of such anxiety-reducing moves is the separation of the nature of the truth given to the church from its content. Surely the content is theological. But the very word "theology" raises the specters of Doctrine and Dogma, and intellectuals in the church worry anew over the possibility of thus being put back into making Christian truth-claims. So theology becomes an objective ("scientific") description of the historic faith of the church, a program offered with many a chaste disavowal of any guesswork as to whether any of it might turn out to be true. Or theology is converted into a philosophical explanation of why religious people persist in talking symbolically if not mythologically. This interpretation of theology allows a hint or two about the reality so represented. For others theology is a delineation of how culture persists in being religious in its literature, painting, politics, etc.

These theological programs can be prosecuted without any significant reference to the worship of the church or otherwise to the concrete and practical Christian life except for purposes of illustration. This does not of course render any of them philosophically invalid. Nor does it reduce their various plausibilities as ways of making Christianity intellectually respectable. Quite to the contrary. Any interpretation of the Christian message that at once leaves the accepted articles of cognition intact and encourages the writing of large drafts upon idealities other than truth is bound to be well received in the courts of the university, the more so if Christian piety is represented as a complex of historical accidents speciously dignified by fantastic theological explanations.

Such piety-denaturing theological programs are embraced with great devotion in the university chapel. There one is invited, if not commanded, to concentrate upon what matters most. Another time and place are provided for such matters as sociological-historical theories about religion, and for psychological-philosophical theories about man, and for philosophical theories about language. There is no salvation to be expected from such inquiries, no matter what facts they uncover and illuminate.

Who would doubt that? No matter how wildly interesting

157

religious behavior is, we cannot legitimately draw off norms, either ethical or theological, from descriptions of it. But suppose that scientific descriptions and explanations are used to confirm an antecedent theological judgment, namely, that only a small fraction of the historic Christian church has any right to persist, that is, has a legitimate demand upon our concern and loyalty. Ought we not ask about that antecedent theological judgment?

I have suggested that such a judgment confronts us in the theological separation of the nature of the truth committed to the church from the content of that truth. By nature I mean the remarkable connection between what is to be believed and certain life-performances prescribed as the meaning of belief and not merely as its concomitant. Thus the original Christian education is instruction in the religious life of the Christian community. The religious life is represented as things to be done, to be enacted, and not merely verbally professed and mentally assented to. The meaning of Jesus Christ is, and not merely entails, the life of obedience in prayer and in loving-kindness. To be sure, the same Jesus Christ walked the earth in Galilee and was crucified outside the walls of Jerusalem. He is the Son of God in whom is incarnate the creative principle of the cosmos entire. But the mind flooded with such wonderful terrestrial and cosmic knowledge is not in any degree thereby freed from the practice of prayer or from the most profound and searching concern for humankind. Thus to confess that Jesus is Lord is to see a new shape of things: the everlasting passing away of worlds, dark and terrible though every such death is, is ordered to an ultimate and absolute triumph of divine righteousness. But to confess that Jesus Christ is Lord is also to pray as he commanded and to die as he died if to live requires betrayal of love. This above all else is the good confession of Jesus Christ.

Therefore the church is called upon to preach what is known in this same Jesus Christ. This peculiar truth allows no abstraction from the peculiar life in the church except for purposes that are false if they are not playful. Accordingly the educational activity of the church, its proper teaching, is designed to form the soul for a vocation in the church and in the world. Whatever its concrete details, this vocation is a unique employment of spiritual power for the enhancement of the real community of mankind, as this community is bodied forth in Jesus Christ.

Thus God has not licensed the church to preach the forgiveness of sins as a universal fact of human existence. There is a place in the church for all who confess their sins. But the church cannot offer absolution to those who have no inclination to seek a new life in the community of those who love God more than they hate their own sins and are willing to accept a very demanding regimen whether or not it looks like fun or is an " in " thing. Apart from this, anyone can seek and probably find that special relief from guilt which consists of assigning it to someone else. Within this kind of spirituality Jesus Christ is celebrated as one come from God to take all our guilt away, a heavenly " Ajax " knight. If we accept this outlook, we ought to find Peter's anguished acknowledgment of his sin of betrayal a bit of touching but meaningless histrionics.

How much of the teaching office of the church can be exercised by the college chapel? The question becomes vexatious as soon as we take note of the apparent ease with which the college church abstracts theology from the ordered religious life and fashions its own forms for the Christian life. There are plausible explanations for this situation, of which perhaps the most impressive is the full exposure of the college church to the blasts of philosophical criticism. The college is now the native ground of the " cultured despisers " of the church's historic message and traditional life. Surely some of these critics, or at least some of their students, can be reached by modernizations of the faith that reveal how amazingly secular the living Christ is and how scornful he too is of medieval ecclesiastical panoply and of pietistic usage. God may not be glorified by any of this. Since he may be dead anyway, it is hardly necessary, and it may be indecent, to consult his wishes in the matter. Here below, a sufficiently modern chapel can count on a long-term appointment, if not tenure, not as a protagonist of the church but as a friend of man.

Add to this the fact (as surely many take it to be) that the college no longer conceives itself to be in the business of soul-making, and we have, apparently, all that we need, and perhaps more than we can use, to discredit the cere-monial aspect of Christianity as being entirely secondary, if not offensive, to refined sensibilities.

Here, then, we have reached the point at which the col-lege chapel seems to have the soundest of reasons for becom-ing, for the larger part and ultimately altogether, a theologi-cal discussion center, at least as far as the teaching office is concerned.

It is no part of my vocation to offer policy advice on these matters to persons who may very well be able to get along without it. I must be content with speaking briefly to the principles involved. So I contend: a college that is tradition-ally and habitually committed to the preservation of a chapel as part of her essential structure ought to acknowl-edge the demands of wholeness in Christian observance. I take this to mean that the chapel ought essentially to be a place of worship, and that none of the essential elements of Christian worship ought to be abrogated from its perform-ance. It means also that the primary teaching function of the chapel is training in and for Christian discipleship. Since there is no Christianity in general, such training is of course designed for life in a particular Christian commu-nity. Which one? That one, the college chapel itself, just insofar as it is a real spiritual community, a congregation in which " the mind of Christ " bodily dwells.

III

Now the ecclesiastical thunderclouds gather in such formidable mass that it would be empty pretense to ignore them longer. I shall conclude, therefore, by stating a view of the relation of the Kingdom of Christ to ecclesiastical organization. This view is likely to be an affront of roughly equal magnitude both to antichurch Christians, whose capital is the college, and to ecclesiastical authoritarians. The intention is not to offend for the sake of excitement. But neither ought one to seek to please simply to sustain the delusion that truth is always the silver lining.

Chapter Seven

THE PRESUMPTION OF THE CHAPEL

I

It has been clear from the beginning of this essay that a full-fledged and historically responsible treatment of the doctrine of the church would not be forthcoming and would not be particularly germane to the topic in hand. But it must be just as clear that I have assumed certain things concerning the church. No theologian would say that these assumptions are indisputable, even from the standpoint of faith. I do not intend now to defend these propositions about the church. Rather, I shall proceed to line out certain of these propositions and undertake thereafter to see what light they throw on the situation of the college chapel. It will seem to some, no doubt, that this procedure is entirely characteristic of dogmatic theology. This may in fact be the case. Since this is not the place for a defense of dogmatic theology, I have simply to hope that this theological posture will be Dogmatic rather than dogmatic. Eventually most of us succumb to dogmatism; but generally without the warrant or the objective of Dogma.

II

The first of these propositions concerning the church is that it cannot be identified theologically with an overarching ecclesiastical structure. This is not said to bring to the surface an underlying antipathy toward ecclesiastical structure. Antipathies of this sort are voiced often enough in the college chapel as well as in other courts of spiritual enlightenment. This attitude is part of a long-standing anti-institutionalism that takes many forms outside the religious life as well as in it. Its appearance in the church can therefore be taken to be an aspect of the secularization of the church's own existence. Secularization is not our present concern in discussing the church, even though it is a very popular theological topic at the moment. Our concern is to insist that ecclesiastical structure is best understood as an instrument of communication. The structures of the church, so far as these are available to empirical description, are without exception instrumental in character. Granted, not every empirical description would disclose or catch this. Ecclesiastics act now and then as though this or that structure of the church were clearly self-referencing and self-justified as an end of human conduct. But these same ecclesiastics would also admit, and this without any unusual duress, that everything churchly exists for the glory of God, even though some churchly things are held by them to be literally divine. But they are not thereby stripped of high dignity or of fundamental importance in the providence of God any more than the human body is reduced to meanness or vileness when we see that it is supposed to be " the temple of the Spirit."

There is good reason for making this our first proposition concerning the church. The reason is largely political, but it is still a good one: the denominational fortresses that encircle the campus are much given to representing themselves as the *real* church, in part because they are organically related to a massive overarching ecclesiastical structure; whereas the college chapel stands all by itself, or often tries to. I do not feel either inspired or obligated to discuss such tender political issues in depth, except when it seems necessary to point out how a particular conviction on them may draw its strength from a mistaken view of the church. So we come again to what I take to be a true view of the church: that in all its structures it is an instrument of communication in a threefold way. (1) Through its forms, God speaks his gracious word to the whole world, to the world as such. (2) Through the forms of the church any given congregation speaks to the whole community in Jesus Christ, both to those who live on earth and to those who have become the " invisible company." (3) Through the forms of the church the world as such, " the whole world," may speak to God. Thus the church's life is triply representational, but in none of these representations is the church supposed to make the continuation of its own forms a matter of paramount importance. The church does not live for itself. It lives for God and for the world. This is to say again that the forms do not have a proper life and value of their own. The distinctiveness of that life and value is still to be understood as derived from the purpose of Almighty God. Even if we were to say that the church alone administers salvation, we ought not to suppose that this salvation is its personal property. There is saving Grace. There is no saving church.

Church is also the name for a power structure among other power structures in the world. The churches are in fact power structures of considerable magnitude even in this post-Christian era. Radical theologians spend a good part of their time between denying and decrying this fact. I do not believe that it is theologically profitable to do either. (We might adopt the theological whimsy of referring to the church as power structure as an " it "; and to the church in its proper spiritual intentionality as " she." This would show how easy it is to plug in on the I-Thou, I-it syndrome.)

164

The power is there. It may have diminished. Let properly equipped scientists test that if they are interested. A diminution of the church's power is not necessarily or clearly a good thing. We should be in a sound position to say that it is a good thing only when we have shown the other cards in our hand, and, specifically, when we have made clear whether we think power is a good thing. On that score I contend that the proper expression of the church's instrumentality is incompatible with a renunciation of its power or with any double-mindedness or coyness about the value of power. The reason for putting the claim so strongly is as much ontological as theological. To be is to act or to be capable of acting. Therefore when an agent (either corporate or individual) surrenders power, it must either be a ruse (that is, strategic) or it must be " bad faith " (that is, self-contradiction). Granted, either a corporate or an individual agent may give up one kind of power in order to secure or to expand its grip on another (and presumably higher or greater) power. Thus a man may renounce riches. Another may forswear sexual congress. Another may abdicate a throne. If these things are done in order to quit the world, they are expressions of bad faith. But any of them may be done to enhance the power to act more efficaciously in and for the world. Any of them may be done in order to enrich the world rather than to demonstrate the power of the ego over its own system. Nietzsche did well to howl so ferociously at the crimes committed by self-sacrificing Christian people. He was hardly the discoverer of this moral aberration, this scheming readiness to give up something of self now in order to pick up the winner's purse later on. In order to do what one can do best, what, in Christian language, one has been created to do, one will certainly have to give up other things. But if one finds the joy one ought to find in doing well what one can do best, the things given up can hardly count for much. If indeed they continue to matter greatly, one has, again, fallen into bad faith.

None of this denies that one may be called upon to give up one's very life for the good of others. Yet even here something like the same principle applies and applies decisively: to give up one's life out of love of others is an act of divine grace. To offer freely, though in exquisite pain, what one has, is surely better than having it snatched away, even though the snatching is done while one sleeps. Thus one who takes chances for the sake of others is not so much sacrificing his life as he is seeking to make his life count for the enrichment of the world. Obviously one cannot in good faith do this, or even hope sometime to be able to do it if one hates the world or oneself.

So if it is said to be desirable that the church should again become poor in the world, we must ask what end is in view for this renunciation of power? Is it to display identity with the multitudinous poor of the world? This would be noble. We would begin to pick up overtones of the Kingdom of God in such a plea when the greatly favored in the congregation began not only to step up their monthly contributions to the church but also to pledge every effort to make a larger slice of the tax dollar available for raising up the downtrodden, who are close enough in great numbers to any congregation so that it is not necessary to hire a detective to find them. Thus rightly to minister to the poor the church needs to augment rather than to diminish its power. This does not deny that the church anywhere and everywhere would do well to take a good hard look at its vested interests.

In none of these untimely comments do I intend to blink away the spectacle of ecclesiastical self-aggrandizement as an ever-present sin and temptation. The history of the church, of any church, can be written with the liberal use of these categories. But the world did not need to wait for our contemporary prophets to learn this. Wherever there is power, it can be (is even likely to be) misused. So also for the church. But it does not follow that weakness, smallness, or obscurity is a Christian virtue. Quite to the contrary: the very magnitude of ecclesiastical structure *may* enable it to become a superior instrument of Christian communication. The plenitude of its resources, the variety and severity of its sanctions, and the resoluteness of its leaders may all be employed for the positive purposes of the Divine Kingdom. But only when and where the church is really the church, only when and where the church acts as a whole-bodied agent among the " dominations and principalities of the world."

We come thus to the second disputable proposition about the church. A congregation becomes part of the church of Jesus Christ only by enacting, acting out, the full gospel of the Kingdom of God. In traditional theological language, God the Spirit takes unto himself a body through which to express his love for the world. In more commonplace language, ideals must be given flesh-and-blood immediacy and vividness of life. I do not offer the commonplace language as a fair translation of the theological. God is not an ideal, he is the supreme existent. But as that, as truly God, his life is both fully within and really beyond every concrete realization. His Word (that is, his wholly characteristic and essential action) invades and fills the present moment, but it is also projected over every moment to come. Thus God does not and will not sacrifice immediacy and vividness for the sake of timeless perfection.

It follows from this that the church is really a living body and is the temple of the Spirit only when it is localized and full of idiosyncratic features. I do not mean that this body can be all idiosyncrasy. It is part of an organic world. Its forms are repeated endlessly elsewhere, and the tides on which it moves reach to the boundaries of the cosmos, wherever and whatever they are. But the body of a living spirit is also inalienably individual. Its gestures, especially the most remarkably expressive and communicative, are its own. The language it speaks is a public phenomenon, but the nuances by which the world is enriched and not merely continued are singular achievements. So also for the church. It is part of a purpose and a power that embrace all that is and is to be. But if the church does not have local color, if it does not proclaim and body forth the Word in a response modulated by an acute awareness of the speciality of its immediate environment, the church is an invalid if not a ghost. Really to be the church the congregation must preach the Word to *these* people. These people are part of the human community. Whatever enhances that community will someday enhance them. Whatever diminishes that community will someday depotentialize them. But now it is up to them to learn the particular will of God, that is, how to show forth the love of Christ on this spot. Not to whom, but how.

The immediacy of the life of the church, let us even say the earthiness thereof, is of course an affront to a very pervasive mentality, namely, that being religious is a matter of having a theological-theoretical view of things. To this we must say that a conceptualized content of Christianity, no matter how elegant, is not a viable substitute for concrete engagement in the life of Christian discipleship, any more than a rich philosophy of love is a viable substitute for loving.

" Concrete engagement in the life of Christian discipleship " ought not to be equated with the latest social passion of the college ministers. The social passion must be there. Its validity as witness to the righteousness of God in Jesus Christ cannot be measured in terms of the vehemence and absoluteness with which it is proclaimed from the pulpit. No preacher can claim the warrant of Christ the Lord for saying: Either you identify yourselves with me in this social passion or you are no follower of Christ. This is a sin of presumption. It is likely to gather unto itself a first cousin, self-righteousness.

168

III

There are other presumptions of the chapel that are likely to be prior to this particular one, and these are likely to be the practical presuppositions of a company of other presumptions.

There are two such antecedent presumptions of the chapel.

The first of these is so triumphant a realization of idiosyncrasy that the possibility of being an instrument of communication with the church at large is cut off at the root. When this happens a chapel may go on to achieve an interesting and edifying spirituality. People may find it a stimulating experience or even an exciting one. But when its forms no longer relate the congregation to the whole community in Jesus Christ, it presumes in arrogating to itself the name and sign of Jesus Christ. When both by conscious and by unwitting gestures the congregation is so acutely aware of being just itself that it is very dimly aware of being also something universal, of participating in something which comprises all man's wretchedness and all God's glory, then the chapel is an unruly fragment of the church of Jesus Christ.

The second sin of presumption is apparent when the chapel abstracts the churchly office of teaching from the offices of proclamation and of priesthood. This process of abstraction is not likely to be announced as being what it is. Proclamation and teaching are quietly merged. The priestly office and sound counseling are quietly identified with each other, and the sacramental component of the priesthood of the congregation falls either into desuetude or aesthetic preciousness. What then is left to teach that is distinctively Christian? And under what warrants is this to be taught?

Descriptive answers to these questions can be made out without too much speculation or other difficulty. The answer to the first question — What is left to teach? — is an

169

idealistic world view, now likely to be markedly humanistic. The representation of this outlook as the real gospel is made in Sunday sermons, in extracurricular seminars on contemporary theological thought, and in the discussion of the ethical revolution that now grips American society. The extracurricular seminars are not in a good position and do not commonly drive to obtain a good position from which to delineate theology as a function of the church. The theology is free floating. It is an intellectual exercise calculated to provide information on currently interesting theological postures and programs. It is not theology calculated to develop either range or acuity of theological judgment for the upbuilding of the church. Indeed, part of the attraction of the extracurricular theological seminars is that no religious commitment is presupposed. One need not be anything or anywhere religious, to say nothing of Christian, in order to read and bat Tillich and Bonhoeffer around.

The chapel-sponsored colloquia on the ethical revolution are, again, hardly calculated to show how the faithful Christian makes his moral judgments and defends his commitments. Overall, the objectives appear to be to show how Christian attitudes toward freedom and creativity speak to the ethical dilemmas and opportunities of contemporary existence, once these attitudes are freed from the incrustations of metaphysical doctrine, archaic ceremony, and legalistic morality.

But there is the second question: Under what warrants are these things taught in a chapel that is still professedly Christian? The charismata of the chaplain come to mind. Charismata are causes rather than warrants. The personal charm and rhetorical elegance of the chaplain may indeed be used for the glory of God. Neither of them is an intelligible answer to the question: By what authority is he preaching an ethical humanism as a substitute for the gospel of God in Jesus Christ?

Answers to this question now fill the air, answers that intend to make short work of the whole question of authority. Consider a sample. The historic gospel has been tried and found wanting. It is strictly incompatible with the best of contemporary thinking about man, cosmos, history, language, etc. It is rare that an application of the criterion of incompatibility runs the gamut of available topics of this order. More commonly one or two items are made the paradigmatic cases. But the result is the same — either some indisputable cognitive achievement of modern man or an inextirpable attitude shared by the pacesetters, if not by all, is the power by which the continuity between modern man and traditional Christian man has been destroyed (and a good thing too).

It is not entirely arbitrary to decide to linger briefly over this double answer to the question of authority for preaching a new gospel in the old chapel. What I have in mind in pausing to reflect on this ought to be put as unequivocally as possible. Thus: " the double answer " actually requires a decision, because the appeal to a cognitive warrant is different from an appeal to an attitudinal warrant. One may of course decide for both, as one tries to make sense out of the gospel for the benefit of a congregation that does not have a common mind as to whether God exists. One may, that is, as preacher in the chapel, point to a decisive cognitive achievement of the modern world and say that is why I am rewriting the gospel for our common benefit. More precisely, to what might one point? Let us use proper names to answer that question. Freud? Einstein? Skinner? Ayer? Hoyle? Sartre? Marx? If the preacher in the chapel, or the informal theologian in the extracurricular classroom, is making the cognitive appeal, then we have the right to ask him for the cognitive hero, and not for an attitude emanating therefrom but for the advancement of knowledge that puts the old gospel out of the court of truth.

I admit that this is, for working purposes, a brutally unfair question. Where is the chaplain sufficiently competent in cognitive affairs, as these are widely understood in the university, to stake out such a claim and provide a respectable defense of it? The chances are rather high that if he had such competence, he would not be a chaplain. What he does, therefore, is to take it on extrinsic authority that such and such is an authentic cognitive achievement and thereupon undertakes to draw a series of negative inferences for the proclamation of the historic gospel. He appeals, that is, not to what he knows but to what is reported to be known.

It is therefore little to be wondered at that the sharpness of the decision, *either* cognitive *or* attitudinal, is so often dulled or evaded. What has happened is that the chaplain has become in himself a paradigm: he has a reverential attitude toward the cognitive heroes and/or to the cognitive community at large. That community is at once an empirical consensus of learned judgment about empirical states of affairs, a value system, and an attitudinal posture. Thus he speaks for himself when he discourses from the pulpit on the life-attitudes of modern man which demand the radical revision of the gospel of Jesus Christ. Man has learned to do a great many things for himself for which in dimmer ages he looked for help to heavenly or anyway divine powers. What he needs now is a Friend. He does not want a Judge; he has learned that guilt is a bad thing. He cannot have a Creator; he has learned from Einstein (or was it Bondi or Hoyle?) that he does not have one, and from Freud that it is pretty sick to ask for one. A Redeemer would be nice to have, but what remains for a full-time Redeemer to do? But still a Friend would be great: one who feels with us every triumph and every disaster and who himself is (was) demonstrably righteous enough to make reliance on his counsel a wise thing.

How is it possible to cash attitudinal generalizations and prescriptions (or recommendations) into theological decisions and theological arguments? I cheerfully admit I do not know the answer, except to say that it is being done.

Superficially it appears to me that learning what attitudes prevail in a segment of society, or in society at large, would be a job for sociologists rather than for preachers or theologians. But now suppose that this job has been adequately done and we have the announced results in hand. Does the preacher of the gospel have any critical comment to offer on these prevailing attitudes? Ought people to feel the way they apparently do? Ought they to act on the basis, at the behest, of prevailing attitudes? If the preacher has no such critical comment, he has nothing to preach. He is then a reporter, at secondhand, of the empirical state of affairs. By casting his report in autobiographical terms, he can make a dramatic account. He can tell others what he is doing in such a world. He can testify that in doing this he feels that he enjoys the friendship of Jesus. He can welcome others to this enjoyment, or at least to try for it. And for this purpose he can construct his own mythology. Indeed, since he has constructed his own Christology, he had better build or borrow a mythology to support it.

It is time to state flatly the theological conviction that lies behind these intemperate remarks on the abstracted teaching office of the college chapel. This is the principle: the Kingdom of God, revealed in Jesus Christ, does not come into view as the object of the highest devotion, as the end worthy of unreserved commitment, so long as we allow ourselves to swim in an artificial pond of sociological conjectures, philosophical theories, and commitments to freedom and creativity that are either abstract or ego-referencing and ego-justifying. The Kingdom of God comes into view as an object of highest devotion in the person of Jesus Christ. This Person is known for who he is, and loved for who he is, only in the whole church.

The " whole church " does not refer to a worldwide ecclesiastical structure. The whole church exists wherever a congregation gives itself altogether to the celebration of the beauty of God and to obey the revealed Lord.

IV

Given this principle, we cannot reasonably evade an in ference of grave practical import. No decree of heaven or law of history demands that the chapel must fall into presumption and therefore become a fragment of the church, alternatingly vibrant, shrill, and anxious. Having fallen into presumption, the chapel may be redeemed from that condition and bring forth fruits worthy of repentance.

This is to say that the chapel can become a congregation in Jesus Christ. I do not put it this way to give undue value to human religious aspiration. The proper emphasis falls, instead, upon the prevenient readiness of God to create wholeness in the body of his own choosing.

Moreover, the chapel does not need to petition some ecclesiastical main office in order to become a congregation in Jesus Christ, a member of the whole church, an embodiment of the whole church. If it is filled with the grace of wholeness of life, a congregation will naturally (indeed, irresistibly) seek to give its own instrumentalities the widest scope possible as well as the greatest intensity of immediate application. So long as the chapel does not prize its individuality above the Kingdom of God and does not condemn either the splendid or the dim parish church, it enjoys a properly spiritual freedom to relate itself to ecclesiastical structure as it sees fit. Having come under the affirmative judgment of God in Christ, the congregation must seek an appropriate way of showing its redeemed love of the world. It cannot do this by playing spiritual games in a closet. But how it is to be done can be determined only by " prayer and fasting," only by the most rigorous expression of corporate responsibility.

Theologically we say that a chapel (or any other congregation, for that matter) becomes the whole church only under the presence and tutelage of the Holy Spirit. What then are some of the signs of the Spirit? (We ask for the sake

174

of recognitions rather than for the sake of predictions.)

The first answer to this is general. The second is a specific reference to the situation of the college chapel.

The Holy Spirit is at work generating a congregation in Jesus Christ when people together become ready to accept both a corporate and an individual regimen of prayer and of work. Not prayer *or* work (the works of love). Prayer *and* work. Except in a purely sociological sense, a congregation cannot become a church in Jesus Christ apart from a regimen of prayer. Where this regimen is ordered by the Holy Spirit it includes the whole range of the life of prayer. Without this life of prayer an assemblage of religious people is fatally prone to make the work of the gospel into works-righteousness. Of course other people may benefit from this. In any case there is nothing sinister about good people coming together to be reminded that they are good people. But this coming together has nothing to do with the life in Christ, who after all did command his followers to pray without ceasing.

The Holy Spirit is at work generating a whole church wherever an assemblage of people (who indeed may have come together mostly out of habit) begin to seek a unity and concreteness of action in the name of Christ exactly where they are in the world. This is not incompatible with world outreach. Rather, it is a test to determine whether this assemblage, this congregation, is a living body as well as a lofty mind. Thus in the chapel we have to ask ourselves (and believe it is the Word of God that informs both the question and the answer) whether we are enacting the Gospel, living the Kingdom of God, as a body and as a distinctive company. I suspect that so many chapels have " associate memberships " for reasons other than tender regard for denominational sensitivities and, specifically, because there is nothing visible in the chapel that would require full membership, undivided attention, whole presence. If such is wanting, the chapel has no choice but to remain a frag-

175

ment. But also if such is wanting, we are up against our own dimness, sloth, or pride, in not amending this condition.

Ideally, we are now ready for the more particular answer to the question concerning the signs of the Spirit. The Spirit is present when the chapel manifests a readiness to live in the university and in the surrounding community as a representative of the Kingdom of Christ rather than as a colony of an ecclesiastical empire.

Here again we are likely to receive severe nudges from the political problems. If the university pays the bills for the chapel, the chapel may succumb to one set of establishmentarian diseases. If the denomination pays the bills, behold! another species of locust darkens the sun. But suppose that in the main the chapel were to become self-supporting. Suppose that this is one of the ways in which the congregation could accept responsibility for its distinctive existence — even if it meant paying rent to the university for the use of a building. As it is, the congregation is asked to support the " outreach," this or that special project, the spiritual and ethical luxuries. The congregation does not have to pay for the privilege of being itself. It is sponsored. It does not need to go without a meal. Perhaps that is why the Lord's Supper is an expendable in the chapel, arranged so tastefully that the unbelievers can make a graceful exit while the traditionalists hang around to play church. Or put it theologically. The Supper of the Lord is for the hungry, for the really hungry, those who know what it means to have an empty belly and no manna in sight. So how can even Almighty God consecrate such stuff as cheap wine and gritty bread for the benefit of people who are dedicated to eating themselves into cardiovascular disasters while uncounted millions are starving to death? Well, he does. The Lord's Supper is truly a miracle, no matter what the chapel devises.

There is a corollary to the particular sign of the Spirit with which we are concluding. The Spirit is working to lift an assemblage of more or less religious people into a congregation in Jesus Christ when in it a readiness develops to admit that chapel, with all its loveliness, is not the only structure congenial to the Kingdom.

I hope that this is not an unduly negative note on which to conclude. Certainly the intent is not negative. It is the case that for some students — and some is too many — any other kind of churchly existence, and any other kind of ministry, becomes unthinkable. What can the dimmer kind of parish church offer them? Wretched music. Even worse architecture. Ladies' aid societies. Low-grade preaching, low-grade as well as old-fashioned. Sunday schools. Church picnics. Bishops with the souls and manners of Marine sergeants. Budget problems. All of this is the *real* church? Oh, for those wonderful Sunday mornings in the chapel — the music, the preaching, the coffee-hour theology, the seemly congregation!

Bad architecture, poor sermons, officious women, obnoxious ecclesiastical overlords, etc. — none of these is a mark of the real church. All are expendable, or at least amendable. But not for the sake of spiritual preciousness. Not for the sake of a disembodied religiousness. Not for the sake of prettiness or breathless contemporaneity. The self-congratulatory flourishes of the chapel are more comfortable but they are not nearer the service of the Kingdom than all of these abominations of the parish church. That too is vulnerable to the prevenient grace of God. That too can be lifted into the wholeness and purity of the love of Christ.

VI

As in the beginning, so at the end. I do not profess to know where the Christian college is going. I have presumed to express only some convictions concerning where it ought to go, what it ought to do, to remain or to become really Christian. Those who do not want it to remain or to become that have not received much of my attention in this essay.

177

That is simply because this essay is not itself an effort to make a case for Christianity. I think such a case can be made. I think that even a nominally Christian institution of higher learning is an excellent place to make it, to test it, to act it out. This cannot be done by a vote of the trustees. It cannot be done by a vote of the faculty. The student self-government organization cannot bring it to pass by a vote. (These are listed in the order of diminishing plausibility.) But that peculiar assemblage which is the college chapel can move up as a congregation into the range of churchly existence and thus embody, show forth, act out, what the argument is about. So again: the congregation of the faithful does not exist in order to prove that God exists. It exists to serve him. But it is one of the most delicious paradoxes in the university of our time that formal theologians in the main offer religious excuses for leaving the " God question " to the philosophy department. I find my confidence in the divine Providence strengthened whenever I contemplate the fact that philosophy departments have people who are ready again to take up the question. Not, of course, to serve the church. Or to praise him. But because the big questions will not stay down. Perhaps in that they are like a bad dinner. But perhaps in that they are rather like reality itself.

Chapter Eight

LITURGY AND POLITICS

I

One of the traditional functions of the church in the university is to provide for the public worship of God. Perhaps the most exalted — or most grandiose — description of the chapel is " the university at its prayers." Surely in this respect chapel *is* church rather than a fragment of the real article, because the worship of God is close to the heart of the church's reason for existence.

The university chapel as a center for worship is exposed to a wide variety of criticism. Guns on the left bark objection to the persistence of any archaic ritual — prayers, the Lord's Supper, confession, etc. From the right comes fire aimed at the presumption of the chapel in making any traditional sacramental gestures. The center attacks the substitution in liturgical matters of aesthetical whims, theological hunches, and prophetic passion for clear cogent principle.

So far as I can see, the chapel line is not dramatically crumbling under these attacks. Perhaps this is the case because they converge accidentally. But the friends and leaders of the chapel may also feel reinforced by the movement of denominational campus ministries into the chapel position. Whether or not this is powerful support for the chapel, one

ought to ask what accounts for this movement. Some answers are always at hand, such as the attraction of a fully
licensed university operation, with all the rights and privileges appertaining thereto, for brethren who have hitherto
been condemned to peripheral status. A rather different answer, however, might be made out. I shall state it and then
suggest what is required to make it stick.

The university chapel is a presiding genius in the liquidation of traditional liturgical forms. At the moment (and one
could reasonably predict that this will continue), the chapel
is also a severely idealistic critic of the political order. I do
not see many clear indications that the people of the chapel
are thinking hard or well about the interconnections between these two things. But surely the resources for that are
at least as available in the university chapel as in denominational structures.

Thus the chapel is emerging as the Christian center
closest to the "action." That would seem to make it the
choicest strategic base for launching a reconstruction of the
liturgical life of the faithful.

Now what is required to make this answer really stick?

1. An exploration of the interconnections of the political
and liturgical orders. It is not hard to credit the claim that
the old alliances between religion and politics are either
dead or mischievous. But the very existence of the university
chapel argues the viability of some intimate connection of
the liturgical with the political order.

2. A fresh attack upon the ambiguities of Christian ethical concern. These ambiguities flourish in myriad forms
where the Christian must take one position or another in
the political order and appraise decisions made for and by
him. Accordingly the church is caught in the tension between accusative and justificatory pieties. The university
chapel is anything but an exception to this, despite a concentration upon the accusative severe enough to stir a sus-
picion that the last residue of justificatory piety is being cut

away. In the chapel one hears truly remarkable expansions of the accusative mode, but the depth dive into unconscious guilt is a prime specimen of a justificatory-expiative gesture.

3. Renewal of worship. Creative reconstruction of the liturgical-political order neither begins nor ends with programs for " enriching worship." On the other hand, the prayers and hymns of the people, both in and outside the context of the sacraments, are certainly more than frosting on a theological-ethical cake. There must be some instruction in the fact that here the university chapel walks as falteringly as does the church elsewhere. Most of its iconoclastic gestures are puerile. Most of its positive innovations are aesthetically trivial and theologically capricious. Renewal of worship, indeed! For this the people of the chapel ought to add their prayers to those of the church generally.

II

Before proceeding into other features of 1, above, I want to sketch several varieties of liturgical-political order. The phrase " liturgical-political order " is used to suggest an interlocking of the realms of religion and politics, so that the function of liturgy is not so much to dramatize the intramural life of the church as it is to show God, piercing and claiming the powers of the world for his purpose.

Thus the corporate life of Israel in Old Testament history is a liturgical order. In the faith of Israel the very sense of life is informed and suffused with the mysterious righteousness of the Lord. This does not mean that God is seen in all things and heard in every voice. Rather, nothing escapes his knowing or threatens his purpose. This Lord has made known how the life of his people is to be ordered. Therefore, going up to the Temple and observing seasons and days are important, but they are not salvific of themselves. Only the Lord is strong to save. He has saved, he will save. Therefore praise him, and in every vicissitude — and he ordains an incredible variety of them — hold fast to the hope that never betrays, and in all things about which he cares, care to do his will.

A very different kind of liturgical order is manifested in the tragic drama of Hellenism. There we see that the gods take an interest in human life. But they care variously indeed. It is almost as though the vagaries of mortal life, the same being inescapable no matter what one's religion, are reflected faithfully in the whimsies of immortal powers. Or is it the other way around? No doubt the issue is theologically momentous. The liturgical order does not wait upon the outcome. What appears to be raw contingency, sheer chance, fantastic coincidence — all of that is the bewildering disguise of necessity. The sportive gods themselves cannot break out of that order. The great liturgical question is whether even the sublime high gods, those superb avatars of wisdom and beauty, can render the iron divine order humane and benign.

Given this vision of its cosmic context, what is the proper ordering of human life? One that respects the divine ordination of boundaries, limits, and natures. So even that benign god, Reason, seeks not to change things but to comprehend what they are. Thereby life can be delivered from servitude to the illusions that breed Hubris which in turn leads men to test the divine order and bring ruin down upon them.

The differences between these two liturgical orders, Israel and Hellas, are great. Yet in one vital particular they are close relatives. For neither is the main fabric of human life constituted independently of the ultimate power celebrated in the cult. So for neither is liturgy a collection of odd dispensable things performed at spare-time intervals in the corporate life. The essential meaning of the life of the people or of the city is expressed in the liturgical order.

The liturgies are very different from each other; so are the conceptions and realizations of political order. On the latter we ought to resist the temptation to construe the prime difference as a ready disposition in the Greeks to make something godlike of their kings where the people of Israel were spared that political-theological error. Israel came in due time to reject all deifications of the creaturely and specifically of the human. But the record of the tragedies is in its way just as clear as the Old Testament: hero-kings (not all heroes are kings/not all kings are heroes) are larger than life but they are spared none of its suffering. Least of all are they spared the awful consequences of overweening pride. In fact, *that* suffering is paradigmatic for the whole state. Tragedy is therefore a cautionary tale for king and commoner alike.

Hellas and Israel are then two realizations of political order responsive to an overriding, overarching moral order. Hellas reads that moral canopy, beneath which all momentous affairs of state pursue a prefigured course, pretty much as an eternal intelligible order. Israel hears it as the word of a living and jealous Lord.

For various reasons Hellas gave a value to political order that Israel did not, and indeed could not, match. Even so the last and greatest word of Hellenic life on the subject of politics, Aristotle's, reveals an intimate connection with the liturgical order still intact. He did not expect that rulers would be godly men. If they are wise and just, the state will prosper until its license expires. The acquisition of such virtues is not an accident. Theology plays an important role in the discipline requisite for leadership of public affairs.

American theocracy as a liturgical-political order is of course much nearer to us than Israel and Hellas. Radical critics of contemporary society are prone to make Puritanism a master villain. Revisionist piety in the university chapel shares much of that animus. I am not concerned, nor am I competent, to appraise the historical validity of such accusations. It is more important that certain remarkable features of the Puritan liturgical-political order not be neglected.

One of these is a conviction that the New World is the

scene in which a covenanted people will create on earth a faithful reflection of the Kingdom of God in heaven. Spiritually armed with this conviction the Puritan clan faced the threats of the howling wilderness with indomitable courage and patience. Almighty God would not have brought them hither to die fruitlessly. Many did die betimes; but the righteous and Godly company endured and at last prevailed.

That was not just good luck. " Luck " was not in the Puritan theological vocabulary. God's gracious sovereign hand had done it. Very well. But the providential divine order surely does not penalize human political ingenuity. The theocratic community in New England was a small masterpiece of that: the self-government of the village was a faithful political reflection of the self-discipline of the Christian, a pilgrim in a world harshly inimical to the health of his immortal soul.

Another element of note in the Puritan liturgical-political order is to be found in the quality of worship in which that order is celebrated. I refer here not to its legendary austerity (austerity is the enemy of self-indulgence and trivializing; it is not the enemy of aesthetic elegance) , but to the high importance the Puritans attached to doing things in good order. No more here than in anything else did they suffer chance or whim gladly. Their hymns, homilies, and prayers radiate unbrookable confidence in the great destiny on earth and in heaven to which God has called them. That bright vision is as much and as truly the criterion for a correct assessment of human character and performance as any dark theological presumption that human life is burdened with humanly inexpiable guilt.

A third feature of the Puritan liturgical-political order could be projected from what we have reviewed so far. It does not allow a separation of the political realm from the religious. Expressed positively, the governance of the state is as much within the direct providence of divine calling as, say, the preaching of the gospel. As it worked out this meant

184

that moral excellence of character was an indispensable qualification for political leadership. It was not the Puritans' fault that "moral excellence" came in American life generally to denote the virtues of the interior life. It is notoriously difficult to translate such into qualities of character capable of managing large, complex, and hazardous public matters for the benefit of all.

The plays of Shakespeare present a liturgical-political order different from any sketched so far. I discuss it here because it has long penetrated American theology of politics without regard to antiquarian interests, literary or otherwise.

Shakespeare knew enough about the history of England and about human nature to reject any temptation — chauvinistic, partisan, or theological — to represent the ruler as a man of preeminent righteousness, to say nothing of holiness. The seventeenth century saw a remarkable theological-political innovation called the divine right of kings. Shakespeare is mercifully free of the taint of that heresy. Who challenges the king does not *eo ipso* challenge God. He depicts all too clearly how kings are made and undone. With us they are made to know what fragile and corruptible stuff all their power and pomp is.

Nonetheless the governance of the state calls for wisdom and compassion beyond common attainment anywhere. When they are lacking, the body politic sickens. Shakespeare's princes do not petition heaven for these graces. But when the ruler falls, whether from ineptitude or his own folly or the ambitions of other men, he may well recognize the magnitude of his failure: not merely that his own person is now in mortal jeopardy but that the nation is endangered.

If the onetime king is not capable of acknowledging the proper dimensions and cause of his failure, Shakespeare provides characters who can and do. They are likely to take the next step, namely, to shore up the sagging walls of the

185

state. Thus in *King Lear* when the cup of tragedy overflows
and all are about to be inundated by boundless horror and
pity, there is a sharp recalling to the affairs of state — and
on that note the play ends.

At that point we have *not* been returned to a capping
cliché, " Life goes on." It does of course go on, but to ob-
serve or assert that is no business of high art or serious religion. Shakespeare is saying that the political order has an
authoritative claim upon the affections and loyalty of its
people. This claim is such that private emotion must give
place to the grand public affections on the strength and purity of which the state is able to endure. The drama itself has
an important liturgical function right here. Playing upon
either historical or fictive occasions, it focuses heart and
mind upon the present moment in the destiny-stressed history of this England, and to pungent fears, as well as to
lambent hopes, it gives immortal expression. That is liturgy,
whatever names of God are intoned in it.

The Shakespearean account of the liturgical-political order has taken up life far beyond the boundaries of Elizabe-
than art and English history. Notably for our purpose it has
produced modulations in the Puritan order: America is an
" almost chosen people " rather than a folk upon whom
God has inscribed a clear and invincible election. Kings are
clay and irresolute spirit; but the death of a king calls for a
display of public emotion, whatever the cost to private comfort, for the nation can claim its destiny only if it claims a
place second only to God in the affections of its people.

III

There may be something in modern experience that sys-
tematically rejects all the historic patterns in which the
liturgical and the political have been woven together. I suppose that the theological call for a " desacralization of politics " is an affirmative response to such a factor in the modern mind. This seems to promise more than a thorough

stripping away of pseudo-mystery from the political order. What more? Is the target, perhaps, the transcendent rather than the sacred? This is not implausible because a transcendent moral Will is still ritualistically invoked on state occasions. But is this to be opposed because it is a stale gesture or because it excites dubious theological passions? The remedy for a stale gesture is a new one. Theological passions that offend normative sensibilities ought to be jettisoned rather than resymbolized.

So again we must ask whether " the desacralization of politics " pleads for a complete domestication of every value factor within the human commonwealth, and beyond that for reducing transcendence — one of the most obdurate of theological passions — to a quality of human interests. Is this, moreover, the direction to which " normative sensibilities " incline?

The latter question is difficult to answer because we are not sure that the attack on theological passions is itself theological rather than biographical and sociological. Sociology hardly breathes the air of " normative sensibilities." From the fact that x number of people say they do not believe or otherwise appreciate p, it does not follow that p ought not to be believed or esteemed, even if x is a very large number.

Though we are uncertain about much of the business into which we ought to be put by " normative sensibility," we can be reasonably certain about some of it. The manageable part is an appeal to idealities. Furthermore, we can be sure that every such appeal will be shabbily treated both by unleavened masses and by self-certified cultural elites. Happily for mankind, ideals are not thus invalidated.

So if the liturgical-political invocation of a transcendent realm were consistently to be understood as an expression of an idealistic commitment, it might be acceptable to normative modernity. This assumes that the best of modern spirituality is itself oriented to an inclusive ethical commonwealth, overarching national, ethnic, and religious boundaries. That order is not identifiable with any empirical state of affairs. It ought to be but is not except as a claim upon hope, faith, and love.

Responses of the university chapel to recent developments in national politics provide interesting clues to directions in which reconstruction of liturgical-political order is moving. In the chapel idealism has assumed cultic form. It is hard even to remember clearly when Puritan pietism and moralism last commanded a flow of accusative rhetoric. That rhetoric is now a vivid tide swirling destructively around every footing of the System.

On the positive side the idealistic reconstruction is producing its own heroes, saints and prophets, and bands of totally dedicated followers. Among its master heroes there is a knight *sans peur et reproche.* He valiantly attacks the entrenched forces of the political system and he does this without thought of gain for himself. His appearance on the scene is mysterious, providential. Coming out of nowhere, and unarmed except for Truth — that " terrible swift sword " which astounds and appalls the System — he reduces a noxious political empire to dust, and legions of its erstwhile prisoners rise up and gladly follow him toward the light.

The new order also has prophets. It is the calling of the prophet to proclaim the acceptable service of divine righteousness and to point the finger of divine wrath at every obstacle placed by self-serving politicians and their priestly apologists in the path of the innocent.

And the new order has its martyrs: men who preferred to let life be brutally snatched from them rather than to betray the vision of the Great Future.

It would seem a shocking malfeasance of Providence had bands and armies of totally dedicated followers *not* arisen, given such signs and wonders. They have arisen; so that theological scandal has been averted.

What we have here is more than a vigorous high-minded political protest. It is liturgical, incipiently perhaps, but really nonetheless. That is to say, it is a cultic celebration of a moral order that exacts requital for injustice and needless violence. It can be called cultic because the decisive gestures employed have twofold meaning: one for the outer world, the other for the dedicated participant. The latter dimension of meaning runs beyond the " literal " and sets the tone for the whole enterprise.

Another way of describing these cultic features is to say that they are incantational. They are designed to draw into the engagement with evil, moral forces that otherwise would remain slumbrous, dormant, and diffuse.

Thus a significant part of the evil against which the new liturgical-political order marshals the forces of righteousness has a religious quality. It is the idolatrous sanctity that makes our political institutions unresponsive to the demands of justice. The defenders of the System are prone to claim that it is the creation and the guardian of pure religion. Thereby the best of traditional religion in America is irremediably compromised, the sense of a divine righteousness that cannot be drawn into bloody squabbles over human arrangements.

That lofty piety at its best was seriously defective. The God it worshiped was too inscrutable — if inscrutability admits degrees. He reigned in unfathomable righteousness, and his wholly mysterious will was absolute. How could any practical guidance be wrested from such a God? How could belief in such a God be distinguished from any absolute determinism? From such theological schemes one can extract an odd nectar for comfort in tribulation. But how can one even dream of using them — any of them — both to illuminate and reform public policy?

Given these sentiments, these theological and moral passions, it is not so very remarkable that the university chapel has become the context in which an anxious and avid search for an inclusive new piety goes on. A theology adequate to a transcendently idealistic involvement in transforming society, an ethics appropriate for a constituency liberated at last from ancient guilt and fear, worship enriched by the best contemporary art: these are the chief elements of the new liturgical-political order sought by the leading spirits of the chapel.

There is much to commend in this quest. The usages of traditional pieties may be both more durable and more perspicuous than their radical critics in the chapel suppose. Even so, Tradition at its best is a point of departure and not the preeminent criterion. But if Tradition is not the latter, if we really believe that it is not the preeminent criterion, then we should stop using it as an important negative criterion, as a definition of what we certainly do *not* want. For if the past is really dead, we should have simply forgotten it. There is little sense and no salvation in beginning each day with a solemn injunction to forget the past. I suppose, furthermore, that people are helped to forget the past, to overcome it — at least to that degree — by nothing so much as by a strong and clear sense that today and tomorrow they can achieve something significantly new. This sense may be illusory on any given day short of the Eschaton, but this failure cannot be predicted — that is one of the great things about hope.

The quest for a new order can be faulted at another point. Its prophets do not apprehend what the old order tried religiously to cope with. That is a powerful tension in human life created by the inescapable demands of finite order and the inordinate demands of divine righteousness. This tension is the heart of the religious problem.

Hellas did not know this better than Israel; Aristotle or Sophocles better than Moses or Isaiah. Scholarship cannot uncover or re-create the particular intuitions in which each grasped the conflict of finite arrangements with divine righteousness. We can ponder the historical consequences, the religious, political, scientific, poetic, creations designed to make the contrast tolerable and commonsense. We marvel at the *superbia* with which Hellas dreamed of " participating Eternity " by matchless achievements of word and marble. We are sobered by Israel's prayer, " Establish thou the work of our hands, O Lord."

<h2 style="text-align:center">IV</h2>

Whatever the faults of the quest for a new order, we cannot gracefully deprecate or overlook the manifest seriousness of the chapel in exposing the ambiguity of the church's ethical concerns. I believe that this ambiguity is generated in part by a persistent sense of that agelong tension previously referred to. But I think that this sense has lost much of its vividness. The Standard Package of contemporary (American) life seems in fact to be a denial of that tension. The man " who has it made " has met all the important expectations both of man and of God. The righteousness of God offers no threat to the perfection of his self-esteem. Daily he looks upon his creation, himself to wit, and finds it very good. No wonder he is a supersalesman for the Standard Package.

This is a caricature whether or not that parody of the good man, the man who has it made, knows it. For the Standard Package includes a wide assortment of anodynes. Some of these are innocent nostrums. Others are as deadly as the evils they are concocted to relieve. None would be necessary if all the winds were fair and all the shores were hospitable. Only the most insensitive — from birth or from perverse habituation — can believe that. For the rest the Standard Package is as much a survival kit as it is a foolproof recipe for the good life.

In the church the gospel is often handed out as part of the Standard Package. It is something God himself has pre-

191

scribed to be taken with one's favorite beverage whenever the world — or one's very own self — threatens to become too much for one.

The accusative rhetoric of the chapel has a fat easy target in this corruption of the gospel of divine reconciliation. Zeal in flaying it may lead one to believe that white middle-class citizens (to say nothing of the hedonistic parasites at the top of the heap) have lost every prospect for the divine Kingdom, and that the church, because it has issued countless counterfeits, has lost the true Keys of the Kingdom. So what the chapel now binds on earth shall be bound also in heaven, or heaven too will be liquidated. All of which goes to show that accusation has a certain affinity with hyperbole.

There is a rather more sinewy and dexterous form in which the ambiguity of Christian ethical concerns is encountered in both the church and the chapel. Rightly to be critical of this form, the chapel must then learn to be critical of itself. Hyperbole is not entirely comfortable in self-accusation.

This tougher interpretation of ethical ambiguity runs as follows. The ethical life of the church and the Christian is bound to be ambiguous because the contemporary world is demonically complex. Our madding world does not allow simple good or simple evil. Some shade of ethical gray, muddy, nondescript, or bold, is all it will afford.

Given this sense of the world, we should expect to find reconciliation for it in a liturgical-political order. One of the grand functions of such an order is to do just that: It is a human creation designed to tame guilt, modulate anxiety, and proportion hope to descriable possibility. Guilt, anxiety, and hope all convey a sense of God's inordinate demands.

The ethical complexity of the world produces a superabundance of guilt. Liberal revisions of the received liturgical-political order are largely inspired to cope with that. The quest for a radically new order shares that aim. Both look for a way to reduce guilt for the immensity of needless suffering in the world. From the simple fact of being present in this corporate life, I garner an infinity of guilt. This is to say that the I who is the moral agent clearly responsible as the cause of a, b, c, etc., and the I who is the moral patient engulfed in vast social forces causing A, B, C, etc., are bound into an ethically unmanageable unit. I am not flying the planes dropping hellish death fire on innocent Vietnamese; but they are American planes, and I am an American. Therefore I have guilt transcending my power to cope with it. I did not lock my Afro-American brothers in the ghetto and throw away the key; but that is the American System, and I am an American. Therefore I am infinitely guilty.

The emerging liturgical order goes beyond the best efforts of the liberal system to tame this infinity of guilt. Now we are summoned to acknowledge our *unconscious* corporate guilt. Once it was deemed sufficient to confess one's witting but unavoidable complicity in social evils. Now we are convicted of secret longings for the perpetuation of those evils, longings so horrid that we force them down into the unconscious.

But this must be seen in its close relations with a second liturgical innovation. That is a gesture symbolically canceling the wall of alienation: I freely submit to being raped in one sense or another by the systematic victim of rape. This liturgical gesture must be held in the closest possible relation to a third one. That is unreserved participation in the idealistic crusade against the whole damning and damnable System but particularly against its political idols and overlords.

The second prime objective of liturgical order is the modulation of anxiety. Human societies generally have in their prehistory an active ingredient of anxiety. That is why every success in assuaging and subduing anxiety may well occasion new outbreaks of it. That is why one must think of modulating anxiety rather than of destroying it. For even utopian success in relieving the masses of anxiety will put the masters in the anxious seat. They will not know when the monster, which has slept blissfully for many seasons, will suddenly twitch and spread ruin in every direction or wake up and demand to exchange pleasure for power.

The liturgical order emerging in the chapel offers bright promises for fresh modulations of anxiety. In place of the nostrums of self-help blandly tucked into the Standard Package by an apostate church, the prophetic chapel offers the sublime alternative of helping others and especially the alienated others. Wakeful and concerned Christians do not need to be immobilized by anxiety over the dark clouds obscuring truth, beauty, and goodness for so many people. Meaningful action is possible, action that may arrest the awful drift toward destruction. Providentially this kind of political engagement can also arrest or even excise the cancer of anxiety about one's personal significance. The System threatens to swamp the individual moral agent. Have at the System, not with pointless imprecation but with converted and shrewd action: In order to become yourself, you must do for others.

The third prime objective of liturgical order is the proportioning of hope to describable possibility. Here again we find a need as old as human society itself. Always there has been the problem of tying a significant part of imagination to the possible future, which is different from time-free fantasy. If the perils and frustrations of the present are too severe, imagination slips off into fantasy and political creativity is stifled by dull routine. But hope itself becomes a snare and a delusion if it is not tied into describable possibility. It is all very well to say that hope mocks at every rational calculation of probability. Hope nonetheless requires discipline. Exhausted by too many excursions into never-never on tickets issued by anxiety, boredom, or sheer playfulness, hope then has nothing left on which to rise and make great history out of mean occasions.

A liturgical-political order is viable only so far as it provides a normative envisagement of time-bound possibility. That is why so many of these systems appeal ultimately to Revelation, if by that we mean a self-manifested Reality that binds time and creaturely power to itself. For then the possibilities that matter ultimately are descriable only from the ground whereon Revelation sets the people. Given a tribal God, the future is great with the people's aggrandizement: We shall fill the canvas entire. Given a God whose concern ranges in creative solicitude across all of human life and the world, the future is great with the perfection of man: We do not yet know what together we shall become.

For all the liberal emendations of the traditional order, it is still woefully inadequate to the needs of contemporary life. On one side, it unnaturally restricts the images of hope by setting around them an anthropology and a cosmology invalidated by science. And on the other side, it offers a kind of freedom to hope for eternal happiness that makes men indifferent to the problems of this world.

Therefore the chapel of protest promises to become the chapel of reconstruction, and in that latter capacity makes a fresh bid for mastery of the normative envisagement of time-bound possibility. The ethical boundaries of the possible must be thrown far beyond even their liberal definitions because these have been tutored too long and too thoroughly by agelong fears and stale pieties. Prudence and self-interest have been too long in the saddle of national policy. Even if the fabric of society were to be ripped from top to bottom by revolution and the nation should be stripped of its armed might, this would not be an unseemly price to pay for justice and peace, for the System is rotten to the core and the nation owes it to the tribunal of mankind to atone for its horrid crimes afield.

It is silly and perverse to pretend to discover in such rhetoric the signs of a treasonable commitment to inter-

195

national conspiracy. The informing principle here is ideality, a vision of the ideal state of affairs, the sublime commonwealth of free and loving persons. The items of traditional Christian belief that survive in this climate are the ones most suitable to carry idealistic freight, and of these, notably Jesus the Friend of man.

Perhaps this means that the needs of hope have become exorbitant in our world — have, in fact, acquired power to dictate to the past as well as to the present. Indeed one may begin to wonder how else Jesus Christ could so swiftly and surely move back and forth from being a timeless avatar of moral value (Love) to being a lovable hippie-type Palestinian character.

But this too may be cruelly unfair. The desperate political problems of the day have a certain right to preemptive attention. In more tranquil times — if such there are, somewhere ahead — we might feel warranted in trying to straighten out formal theological matters. Now a nation's soul may be lost and thereafter much of the world's body. Is it not then wholly proper to permit the political to dictate all the important terms to the liturgical in the construction of a new order?

I think not. All men die, and nations too. About death the standing problem is not When? But How? A viable liturgical-political order offers a meaningful celebration of death, both that of Everyman and that of empire.

That sort of celebration is hardly possible unless the people for whom the order is created are disposed to see the whole of things comprehended by divine righteousness. I do not find the university chapel excessively eager to get on with this. If this were a theological luxury, one could understand reluctance to enjoy it. But it is not a luxury. It is a bedrock necessity. And as such it cannot be taken for granted.

V

The chapel is teaching the church not to settle for low-lying goals in criticizing the shape and direction of American life. The chapel is also a model of dedication in pursuing an imperatively needed reconstruction of liturgical-political order. Without that the church will continue to live in sterile oscillation between idealistic protest against manifest evil and blushing paralyzing awareness of its own sinfulness. Sporadic revisions of ritual offer no significant relief from this depressing condition.

But church and chapel alike need a more generous platform for reconstruction than the bashfulness of the church and the stridency of the chapel have found. What is needed is a platform that will properly relate: (1) ideal aims, such as Justice and Harmony, to (2) the celebration of God's presence in a mode transcending inordinate demand. But also the relation of (1) to (3) the national covenant must be revised, in order that (4) the worship of Christ as Prophet, Priest, and King may achieve its proper place in the church and in the Christian. Rightly to worship Christ as Prophet, the ethical aims of the state, Justice and Harmony, must be resolutely pursued. Rightly to worship Christ as Priest is to accept God's presence as transcending his own inordinate demands. Rightly to worship Christ as King is to allow that love of which he is paradigm and pioneer to become the ground motive in making the nation responsive to the demands of Justice and Harmony.

1. As a nation we are at the point where the demands of Justice and Harmony are at once exorbitant and inescapable. Thus God in his absolute righteousness governs the world.

It is a momentous theological error to interpret the terrible inordinacy of these demands as a divine penalty for our antecedent indifference to them. Theological primitivism of this sort fills the air. It is an unhappy and illegiti-

197

mate descendant of the Jealous Lord God. Even so, there is a small splinter of truth in it: the success of finite arrangements in producing a modicum of justice may well seduce the beneficiaries of the system into believing that the problem is solved, and thereafter the system will be used to suppress just complaint. But that puts Harmony in jeopardy, for if a man is in every practical respect my slave, my Christian readiness to call him brother is likely to exacerbate rather than to dissolve his alienation.

The demands of Justice are so heavy because even the richest nation in the world cannot do everything needful and good at once. A realistic and reasonable schedule of priorities for the correction of gross inequities is hard to come by. It is many times harder to enforce upon the general will. Unusual gifts of information and imagination are indispensable for the former. Singular courage and great powers of persuasion are necessary for the latter.

Prophetic adumbrations of a new order make much of the imperative need for a new schedule of priorities. Idealistic critics of the national government advocate as part of that the liquidation of every national commitment in Asia except disinterested friendship and best wishes for a happy resolution of problems. No one knows whether such a resolution of the conflict in Vietnam would assure a massive attack on the domestic problems that threaten to make harmony a daydream rather than a descriable possibility. So the question is whether the risk ought not to be taken in full stride toward a just society at home. Singular courage and great powers of persuasion would be necessary to put this across. Prophetic accusation requires the courage part. The persuasion part comes into play in remolding the general will to accept measurable loss of security and comfort for the uplifting of the downtrodden and alienated. Here the question of ground motive becomes decisive.

Reconstruction of the liturgical-political order must, therefore, make much of the conviction that Justice and

Harmony are the vital political content of God's righteousness revealed as inordinate demand. The demand is inordinate because no finite order can encapsulate or domesticate Justice and Harmony. In his righteousness God uncovers, for all with wit to see, the critical flaw in every human arrangement made with an eye to Justice and Harmony. He does not do this with an eye to shriveling every creaturely pretension. His interest is the free flow of life toward ever richer variety. But unlike us he will not sacrifice harmony to variety nor variety to harmony.

Christ as Prophet brings this divine concern into the inner courts of human life. He proclaims a Kingdom of boundless richness on which hope can draw forever without the slightest hint of exhaustion. But it is a Kingdom whose inviolable law shines in unbearable lambency wherever man's self-esteem throttles or corrupts the flow of mercy toward suffering.

2. The gospel which Christianity accepts as Revelation celebrates God's presence in the world in a form transcending inordinate demand. God will not always chide, neither will he remember our iniquities forever. This does not point to some golden far-off time ahead when God will be overtaken by a fit of amiable forgetfulness. Rather, God comes into our affairs as healing Presence. He created mankind to be one body. It *is* therefore one body. But it is a body suffering many lesions. It is afflicted with terrible suppurating wounds. In this condition the parts that by virtue of some magic or other are able to stand themselves complain bitterly about the stench emitted by the rest. Naturally, then, the simple demand of life itself for the health of wholeness is felt as inordinate indeed, a veritable counsel of perfection.

Christ as Priest mediates the divine life for the restoration of health and the beauty of wholeness. He is our justification. In him we accept the law of the Kingdom as a rule of life rather than as a sentence of death and a seal of damnation.

199

The priestly office of Christ has political content: the state cannot legislate mercy, but it can revise the canons of retributive justice with a view to overcoming ancient pseudo-metaphysical distinctions between criminal and sound citizen. Punitive law will stand in the record as long as history runs. But it can be modulated into something humane, restorative, reconstructive. That is mediatorial work. The Christian has excellent reason for accepting it as a proper service of God.

3. Reconstruction of the liturgical-political order must include as a vital and primary element the relationship of the ideal aims of the state to the national covenant. Theologically understood the foundation of this nation is a pledge to Almighty God. Before the law all men shall be equal, and no man shall be forcibly bound to serve another, and every man shall be free to worship and serve God as he sees fit (provided that he does not use his liberty to destroy the rights of others guaranteed by this reign of law).

" Covenant " is a way of interpreting the history and destiny of this nation. The sense of being an " almost chosen people " is manifested at every important juncture, at least down to the recent past. For sober minds this has never meant that we could do no wrong, or that our worst corporate sins were those of primitive well-intentioned innocence. And rightly so. The errors of governments cannot be likened to the destructive accidents of awkward children. A government is ordered to act in the interests of its people. For this end it may rule badly — expensively, carelessly, cruelly, etc. — but it cannot rule accidentally.

One would hardly deny that covenant has, nonetheless, served as excuse for such things as cruel presumption, the violent erasure of human rights, and bland indifference to dreadful exploitation. Of these horrid things it is legitimate and important to ask whether they have been properly confessed, and if not, why not.

At this point, too, the reconstruction of the liturgical or-

200

der is a crying need. For the good confession of sin is no more than begun by public acknowledgment of guilt. Such declaration is best understood as a small down payment or as a rhetorical gesture made to focus attention not primarily upon the sinner's disgrace but upon the objective consequences of his sin. The fact that he feels badly about his behavior is interesting, but it has secondary value. What matters most are restitution to the injured, so far as that is possible (and the opinion of the sinner on *that* is again of secondary value), and thoughtfully proposed amendment of life, so that the same injury shall not befall the same victim again (or his descendants either).

But can the requirements of a good confession be legitimately or helpfully transferred from private person to that public corporation the state? How in the world can a *government* confess its sins?

The principal difficulties in grasping what is at stake here spring from the restriction of confession to feelings of remorse and to rhetorical displays. For on the decisive points, restitution and amendment, a government can indeed "bring forth . . . fruits worthy of repentance."

Nevertheless, we may well wonder whether such action is not very much easier and thus more plausible in international affairs than in domestic ones. How, for example, can the government make amends for the brutal deprivations of basic rights that Negroes have long suffered? Here rhetorical gestures seem more plausible than anything else.

Perhaps we are confused about this by the elevation of an inadequate model. The model ought not to be that of a person giving back something he has gotten illicitly. Reconstruction of the system to give something many of our people have never had — that is what we seek. This calls for a redress of the sovereign will of the people: The powers of the state shall be used to level the barriers, whatever they are, that have defeated fair access to the fundamental rights and goods of this society.

We can predict that a traditional protest will be mounted against any such demand. " You cannot legislate a people into righteousness! " We must say to this venerable bleat:

1. Some laws are more righteous than others, e.g., a law forbidding slavery is better than a law requiring or ordaining it, and this is because freedom is better than slavery.

2. A society that does not make the life of crime, however denoted, unattractive, is not likely to live long or well.

3. The aim of the state is to secure the conditions of Justice for all, whether they are seemly people or not. The state does not aspire to make persons righteous. It exists to enforce the indispensable requirements of a particular covenant, of which none is more fundamental than an even-handed disinterested reign of law.

The worship of Christ as King is germane to much of the foregoing but above all to the principle of the national covenant.

But how? Even though the Christian church long ago appropriated much of the Messianic rhetoric of Israel, it has always had severe difficulties with the grand affirmation of the prophet Isaiah: " And the government shall be upon his shoulder." Today, particularly, Christian people tend to hurry over this to find salvation in: " Wonderful! " " Counselor! " " Prince of Peace! " And even when men felt very sure about the government of Christ in worldly affairs, they were, in fact, clear mostly about the political authority and power of the Christian people or the Christian church.

A different answer can be given to the question about the governance of Christ in and over the national covenant. Let us say first that the Kingship of God's Christ has a magisterial provenance in the commonwealth of man because he is the God-man. He is the Prince of the Kingdom of God. And he is Incarnate God, God domiciled of his free and sovereign choice in this " tabernacle of flesh," in this human history. Thus the power, authority, and law of the Kingdom of God have been implanted in the commonwealth of man, and they will not withdraw, ever.

Secondly, we say that the Kingship of Christ instructs us in the art of governance. He does not tell us how to construct a state. We can learn from him how to order every motive to the governance of love.

This does not mean that men are in Christ obliged to make love the motive in the pursuit of political ambition or in the execution of political responsibilities. Rather, his revelation of love is the ultimate criterion by which motives and performances are to be appraised. Do they build up the common life? If they aim only at reducing damage to the corporate body (and there are times when that is the best that can be done), do they so serve that end that amplification and purification of that life will be possible later?

Thus Christ as King is worshiped when men, already predisposed to govern and be governed humanely, perceive what the model of humanity really is and bend every effort to emulate it. They will oftentimes fail in this. Some of these failures will be the brute issue of unforeseeable events. Some will spring from bad judgment and wayward impulse. The dictate of wisdom is to understand and acknowledge the difference, and to make amends where grievous sin rather than finitude has ruled.

Thirdly, the governance of Christ in and over the national covenant comes to light in the objective disposition resident in that pledge to make all who dwell in this land brothers in the love of that freedom which devotion to justice alone can realize. Thus the wide inequalities of natural gifts are nothing to the point of an objective disposition to guarantee fundamental humanity to all. No law can do that. But that is not the point. The point is a public intention to do that, a promise built into institution and social process. God knows the promise has been violated. But in a larger sense it has not been and will not be violated. God sees to that. Christ, Prince, Son, Savior, enables us to live hopefully with the terrible bright consequences.

VI

The university chapel has an unparalleled opportunity to forge and test reconstructions of the liturgical-political order. What is the university if it is not the unique center of critical conflicts of value systems? Here the pressure of the ideal is keenly felt, not only by the restless young but by everyone who believes in the pursuit of wisdom.

Moreover, the university is swiftly and steadily becoming the laboratory as well as the training ground of public leadership. The art of government has here a paramount claim. It is not the monopoly of political science, God knows. It is a generic and constitutive concern of the whole university.

Finally the chapel has a unique pastoral-priestly responsibility. It is derived in part from the vulnerabilities of its young people. Here an ancient model of Pastor must be questioned all the way into the ground, the picture of the Innocent about to step into a demonically seductive world. The actuality is shockingly different. The world is overflowing with forces dedicated, so to speak, to alienation. It is wrong to cast students as such into the category of the alienated. Alienation is their fate if it be not averted or transformed. Nothing is so effective for that grand, indeed, that divine, purpose as sound preparation to attack the causes of alienation in the world.

The Christian church, in the university and elsewhere, ought to have an answer for the question, " But what is that sound preparation? " At least the text is quoted often enough: " Whosoever shall seek to save his life . . . ." Christian liturgy is built around a ground conception of losing one's life for Christ and the world. Christian life is a political strategy for losing one's life where and when it can do the most for God, for country, and for the commonwealth of man.